BYZANTIUM
GREECE
ASIA MINOR
Crete
Cyprus

MYTHIC PLANTS

Potions and Poisons
from the
Gardens of the Gods

ELLEN ZACHOS

WORKMAN PUBLISHING | NEW YORK

Workman
Workman Publishing
Hachette Book Group, Inc.
1290 Avenue of the Americas
New York, NY 10104
workman.com

Workman is an imprint of Workman Publishing, a division of
Hachette Book Group, Inc. The Workman name and logo are registered
trademarks of Hachette Book Group, Inc.

Design by Reagan Ruff
Cover illustration by Lisel Jane Ashlock
Additional illustrations: ii-graphics/Shutterstock (endpapers); Pixel Embargo/
Shutterstock (p. 75, 105, 133, 174); Shutterstock (entry icons)

Workman books may be purchased in bulk for business, educational,
or promotional use. For information, please contact your local
bookseller or the Hachette Book Group Special Markets Department
at special.markets@hbgusa.com.

Library of Congress Cataloging-in-Publication Data is available.
ISBN 978-1-5235-2439-6
First Edition February 2025

Printed in China on responsibly sourced paper.
10 9 8 7 6 5 4 3 2 1

For John, whose encouragement, tireless research, and fierce opinions made this book more fun to write and more interesting to read. Little did we know, when you gave me my first Theophrastus, that we would end up here.

CONTENTS

Introduction

When Prometheus stole fire from the gods and gave it to mankind, he hid it in a stalk of giant fennel. Ancient Greeks waiting to question the oracles were given cannabis as part of their cleansing rituals. A quince fruit started the Trojan War. The goddess Demeter was so distraught when Hades kidnapped her daughter that she caused winter to blanket the earth, killing all plants.

In Greek mythology, plants were used for tools, intoxication, warfare, food, medicine, magic, and rituals. Some of those plants were real and still exist today; some of them are mythological, with powers we can only imagine. One very special plant was believed to be extinct for millennia, but modern lab techniques, combined with relentless exploration, have led to an intriguing discovery that may rewrite botanical history.

Mythology is fiction. Mostly. The fantastic adventures, the larger-than-life heroes, the epic romances . . . these capture our imaginations. We know they aren't real, but there's a part of us that wants them to be. And often, buried deep inside the mythological details, there's a grain of truth.

There's a reason we read these stories over and over again, thousands of years after they were written. They are compelling, emotional, dramatic, and seductive. They may seem to be about immortals, but at heart they are intensely human, depicting triumph and failure, desire and despair. And when you combine the mythological with something as real and grounded as plants, it makes those original myths ring true.

Exploring these legends through the lens of horticulture brings us closer to understanding why these narratives were so important to the people who created them. Plants bring the stories down to earth. And knowing that some of the plants actually have the powers and properties extolled in the myths makes these accounts more immediate and real. Would you like to use yarrow, like Achilles, to stop a cut from bleeding when you don't have a bandage? Maybe you'll harvest chaste tree fruit, like the Athenian women did, and use them to ease the symptoms of PMS. You may end up planting an entirely mythological garden, filled with herbal remedies, tasty fruit, and beautiful flowers.

Even the entirely fictional plants are interesting. Will you ever cast a spell by throwing a golden apple at your beloved? Probably not. But now that you know it's a thing, don't you want to know more?

Who were the Greek gods?

While the Olympians, so named because most of them lived on Mount Olympus (Hades lived in Hades, another name for the underworld), are the best-known gods of Greek mythology, they were actually the third and fourth generations of immortal beings in the Greek pantheon. In the beginning there were Ouranos and Gaia, i.e., the Heavens and the Earth. Their children, the Titans, included Kronos and Rhea, a pair of married siblings. Kronos castrated his father and took his throne; then, fearing one of his children might do the same to him, he ate each child as soon as it was born. An angry Rhea tricked Kronos by swaddling a stone and presenting it to Kronos as newborn Zeus. Zeus was hidden and raised on the island of Crete and eventually forced his father to vomit up his brothers and sisters, who emerged fully grown and intact. The war of the Titans ensued, which was won by Zeus and his siblings. Kronos was sent to Hades and never heard from again.

Zeus was king of the Olympians. He ruled the Heavens and the Earth with lightning and thunder, and his numerous infidelities (with mortals of both sexes, nymphs, and goddesses) made Hera—his wife and sister—insanely jealous.

His siblings included Hera, goddess of marriage and family, and Zeus's long-suffering and often vengeful wife; Poseidon, god of the ocean; Hades, god of the underworld; Persephone, goddess of the harvest; and

Hestia, the often overlooked goddess of the hearth. Hestia was eventually replaced as an Olympian by Dionysus, god of wine and son of Zeus with the mortal Semele. Aphrodite sprang spontaneously from the foam produced by Ouranos's genitals, after he was castrated by his son Kronos.

The rest of the Olympians were children of the original six. Athena, goddess of war and wisdom, was born from Zeus's head, without input from a mother. Hephaestos, god of fire and metalworking, was born to Hera without input from a father. Ares, god of war, was born of Hera and Zeus. The twins Apollo, god of music and light, and Artemis, goddess of the hunt, were children of Zeus with the Titan Leto. Hermes, the messenger of the gods, was the son of Zeus and Maia, a nymph.

Also immortal, but nowhere near as powerful as the Olympians, were many minor gods and goddesses. The three Fates determined how long mortals would live and under what circumstances they would die. Each of the four winds was a god. Helios was the god of the sun, Selene was the goddess of the moon, and Iris was the goddess of the rainbow. Nemesis was the god of retribution, and Morpheus was the god of dreams. Basically there was a god or goddess for everything.

Some nymphs were immortal, while others were merely long-lived. There were thousands of them, including tree nymphs (dryads), sea nymphs (nereids), freshwater nymphs (naiads), and mountain nymphs (oreads). Some nymphs were tied to a particular place or thing in nature, and when that thing died, so did the nymph. Nymphs were always female, and while they couldn't all make magic on their own, many of them had a direct line of communication with the big twelve.

What makes a hero a hero?

Sometimes the main characters in myths are heroes, not gods. Often a bit of immortal blood ran through the veins of a hero, and while this may have conferred some kind of superpower, it did not make a hero immortal. Any amount of mortal blood in the family tree conferred mortality on subsequent generations. In fact, mortality may be a requirement for being a hero, for it is the combination of heroic deeds and some kind of tragic, perhaps avoidable, death, that makes these stories memorable.

Herakles was the son of Zeus and the human Alcmene. He was most famous for accomplishing the Twelve Labors, seemingly impossible tasks he had to perform to atone for murdering his wife and children. (It wasn't his fault—Hera cursed him with madness.) A demigod by birth, Herakles begged for death after being poisoned by his second wife. He built his own funeral pyre and threw himself upon it to end the pain caused by the poison. Only after he had died did Zeus immortalize Herakles and bring him to Mount Olympus. Herakles had to suffer a painful, mortal death despite his father's immortal blood.

Achilles was the son of the mortal Peleus and Thetis, a sea nymph. Thetis tried to confer immortality on Achilles but because his father was mortal, this was impossible. Achilles knew he was going to die, but unlike most of us, he had a choice as to how. In book 9 of the *Iliad* he tells us that Thetis showed him two possible fates: a short life where "glory never dies" or a long and unremarkable existence. By nature heroic, Achilles chose the path to glory.

Odysseus, on the other hand, was mortal through and through, albeit more clever than most. He conceived of the Trojan horse, slew the Cyclops, and traveled to Hades and back. He could not, however, save his men, and he returned to Ithaka alone, after a ten-year journey. Nor could he save himself. Warned that his death would come from the sea, Odysseus died at the hands of his unknown son (by Circe), who was armed with a spear tipped with the poison of a stingray.

Many Greek heroes were worshipped after they died, with cults formed around their personalities. Shrines were built for Herakles, Achilles, and Odysseus, among others. We still remember them today, but to consider them equal to the gods would certainly incur the wrath of Zeus.

Who wrote these stories?

Many of us were taught that Homer wrote the *Iliad* and the *Odyssey*. We were told he was a blind poet who composed and recited his epic poems, traveling through Greece several hundred years after the Trojan War. Alas, this simplified biography is no longer universally accepted. Today's scholars agree that these epic poems were passed down through the oral tradition, and that multiple poets contributed to them until they were finally written down.

While this may be a question of burning importance for classicists, establishing authorship is less relevant to our exploration of plants in mythology. There are often multiple versions of individual myths, each interesting in its own right. Different authors tell the same story, adding their own spin to a familiar tale. A list of all the authors referred to in this book can be found at the back of the book, along with the titles of their most famous works and the dates they lived.

Speaking of dates, the stories gathered here date primarily from 800 BCE to 200 CE. Just as we divide our modern eras into things like "the industrial revolution," "postwar," and "the information age," we also have names for the different eras of ancient Greece:

» **The Archaic Period** (circa 750–480 BCE) includes the poets Homer and Hesiod. These are foundational authors, credited with establishing the original Greek mythology.

» **The Classical Period** (479–323 BCE) falls between the Persian War and Alexander the Great's invasion of Asia. The most famous Greek writers during this period include the historians Herodotus and Thucydides, and the playwrights Aristophanes, Euripides, Sophocles, and Aeschylus.

» **The Hellenistic Period** (322–31 BCE) begins with the death of Alexander the Great and ends with the Battle of Actium and the collapse of the final existing Hellenistic kingdom (Ptolemaic Egypt, ruled by Cleopatra). The historian Diodorus Siculus wrote his forty-volume *Bibliotheka Historica* during this time, and several Roman authors, like Ovid and Virgil, wrote about Greek mythology during the same era.

These writers not only tell stories, but also give us insight into how the ancient Greeks viewed their mythology. As with any religion, some followers took the stories literally, while others saw them as allegorical. Greek mythology was used to teach lessons, explain the unexplainable, and even to manipulate the population.

Where was ancient Greece?

Today Greece is a small country in the eastern Mediterranean. It's home to more than 10 million people and a vacation spot appreciated by historians, beach lovers, and drinkers of ouzo. But in the first millennium BCE, Greek exploration established colonies throughout the Mediterranean and around the Black Sea. These colonies included, at various times, parts of Italy, France, Spain, Egypt, Turkey, Libya, Yugoslavia, Croatia, Montenegro, Serbia, Albania, Bulgaria, Romania, Macedonia, Georgia, Russia, Ukraine, and Moldova. This was known as *Magna Graecia*, i.e., Greater Greece.

As the populations of Greek city-states grew, people ran out of land to cultivate and places to live. Locations for new colonies were chosen based on which raw materials could be exploited and exported, as well as on strategic placement for safe, long-distance trade routes. Often a city in Greece would send a group of colonists off to establish a new city, which would remain closely tied to its mother city. Those relationships didn't always last. Mother cities required tax payments, military service, and exclusive trade agreements, which often inspired rebellion.

The expanded geographical area of ancient Greece in its prime meant that ancient Greeks had access to many more plants than can be found in Greece today. Valuable plants, like cannabis and silphion, were imported from distant lands; ingredients and recipes for medicines and poisons, like myrrh and nepenthe, were copied from colonized peoples; and herbs and fruits, like sweet apples and quinces, were imported and added to the Greek diet. Considering the vast geographical differences between the steppes of Russia and the Nile Delta, both colonized by Greeks at one time, it's no wonder so many different plants made their way into Greek mythology.

Two more things...

There are never enough pages in a book to include everything, and I haven't been able to include citations for my sources here. But trust me, I've kept track! If anyone is interested in the research, you can find the citations at: mythicplants.com/citations.

Also, the names of places, heroes, and written works in this book are usually spelled the Greek way. Until recently, these spellings were Romanized, but modern transliterations try to come as close as possible to the spellings in the original language. For example, there is no "c" in Greek, so Heracles is Herakles and Ithaca is Ithaka. In instances where I've quoted from older translations, you'll find the outdated, less accurate spellings. I promise it's not as confusing as it sounds.

So sit back and let me tell you a story. Or several stories. About powerful plants from the Gardens of the Gods.

The Original Dysfunctional Family Tree

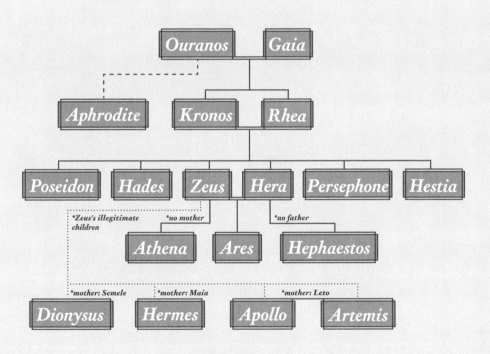

Ouranos — Gaia

Aphrodite

Kronos — Rhea

Poseidon | Hades | Zeus | Hera | Persephone | Hestia

*Zeus's illegitimate children

*no mother

*no father

Athena | Ares | Hephaestos

*mother: Semele

*mother: Maia

*mother: Leto

Dionysus | Hermes | Apollo | Artemis

INTOXICANTS

Grape

Barley

Mandrake

Flying Herbs

Cannabis

Opium Poppy

Grape

Vitis vinifera

While the ancient Greeks enjoyed the occasional grape or raisin as a snack, they mostly cultivated grapes for making wine, which was an essential part of Greek culture, a gift from the god Dionysus. Dionysus has two origin stories. The lesser known casts him as Zagreus, son of Zeus and Persephone (making Zeus both his father and grandfather). In the *Dionysiaca*, Nonnus, a Greek poet from the fifth century CE, describes the seduction. Zeus disguised himself as a dragon and came to Persephone in the night. "He licked the girl's form gently with wooing lips. By this marriage with the heavenly dragon, the womb of Persephone swelled with living fruit, and she bore Zagreus the horned baby." Hera was not pleased and ordered the Titans to chop up Zagreus and eat him, which they did. But Athena stepped in and saved Zagreus's heart, which Zeus somehow magically implanted in the mortal Semele, who gave birth to Dionysus 2.0.

Speaking of Semele, most scholars agree that she was the mother of Dionysus. Once again, Hera was jealous (because Zeus had fathered yet another illegitimate child) and plotted to kill Dionysus. She pretended to befriend Semele and suggested that she should ask Zeus to show himself to her in his true form as a test of his love. Of course, the glory of immortal Zeus was more than poor Semele could stand, and she burst into flames. Zeus ripped Dionysus from her womb at the last possible moment and sewed him up in his thigh until it was time for Dionysus to be born. By doing this, Zeus became both father and mother of Dionysus, making it possible for Dionysus to be fully immortal. Remember, even a drop of mortal blood makes it impossible for the child of a god to be immortal.

Some scholars argue that Dionysus originated in India or Phrygia or Thrace. But evidence from Mycenae shows his name written in Linear B script on clay tablets (the oldest known example of written Greek), proving that he was known as a Greek god at least as early as circa 1400–1200 BCE. He wasn't one of the original twelve Olympians, but several versions of his story say that Hestia (goddess of the hearth) graciously stepped down and gave him her place on Mount Olympus.

So how did Dionysus become the god of wine? The grapevine is named for Ampelos, a Thracian youth whom Dionysus loved. Ovid tells us in *Metamorphoses* that Ampelos died picking grapes, but a more interesting version of this love story is recounted by Nonnus. In his very long poem about Dionysus, he tells us that Ampelos was riding a fierce bull when he insulted Selene, goddess of the moon. She caused the bull to gore him to death. Dionysus was bereft, so much so that Atropos (one of the three Fates who decided how long mortals should live) had pity on him and turned Ampelos into the first grapevine, making him immortal . . . in a way. When Dionysus drank the wine made from Ampelos's vine, he rejoiced, knowing that Ampelos would always be with him. Wine eased Dionysus's sorrow and the sorrows of all who drank it.

Dionysus gave the gift of wine-making to an Athenian named Ikarius who had shown the god hospitality. (Hospitality was *very* important to the ancient Greeks. *See* "Linden.") Ikarius shared his wine with some nearby shepherds, but no one had ever drunk wine before and no one knew what it felt like to be drunk. So when the shepherds became intoxicated, they believed Ikarius had poisoned them, and they killed him.

Perhaps that is why it was considered barbaric to drink full-strength wine in ancient Greece. Wine was almost always diluted with water at varying ratios, most commonly one part wine to three parts water. This made for a much less alcoholic, much less murderous brew.

In the *Odyssey*, Odysseus joins "the men at their wine drinking" and Telemachus invites him to "drink your wine in the men's company." Almost a millennium later, Plutarch, writing about the symposia (famous meetings where Athenians gathered to eat and drink and solve the world's problems), said, "Wine inspirits some men, and raises a confidence and assurance in them, but not such as is haughty and odious, but pleasing and agreeable."

Alas, in ancient Greece, not everyone was allowed to enjoy the gift equally. Greek men believed that women were inclined to drunkenness, and the famous symposia were pretty much male-only affairs. Women were allowed to participate only as servers, prostitutes, entertainers, and flute girls (who were almost exclusively enslaved). As far as the *Odyssey* goes, the closest any woman got to wine was preparing a beverage bowl for her lord and master.

Perhaps if women had been allowed to drink in social contexts, they wouldn't have become maenads, the frenzied followers of Dionysus. You didn't mess with the maenads. These were women who abandoned their womanly duties to follow the god of wine. They drank, they danced ecstatically and sensually, and if you disrespected Dionysus, they wouldn't hesitate to tear you limb from limb.

In addition to being an intoxicant, wine was used medicinally in ancient Greece; the Hippocratic texts prescribed it for multiple uses. Externally it was used to treat wounds and fractures, to make a poultice for hysteria, and to soothe an inflamed rectum. Postpartum diarrhea was treated with a mixture of dark wine, grapes, pomegranate, goat cheese, and flour. Men who wanted to father children were told to drink undiluted, dark wine, but not so much as to get drunk.

The wild grape is native to many parts of Greece, and archaeological evidence dates grapes in Greece to the Pleistocene, which ended

more than eleven thousand years ago. In northern Greece, a series of grape seeds dating from approximately 4500 to 2000 BCE shows the shift from wild grapes to cultivated grapes. Viticulture was well established in Greece during the Bronze Age (approximately 3000 to 1200 BCE). Around 300 BCE, Theophrastus wrote extensively about cultivating grapes, giving readers advice on how to propagate and plant different varieties.

Some modern oenophiles disparage Greek wines, but it was the Greeks who first introduced viticulture to the Romans (by the middle of the second millennium BCE), and then to Marseille (in modern-day France), which the Greeks founded circa 600 BCE. Today Italian and French wines are both far better known, but modern Greek wines are gaining recognition and respect. Several millennia-old Greek grape varietals are being used to make modern, award-winning wines, and countries including South Africa, Australia, and Italy are planting these same varieties of grapes. You can even buy yourself a bottle of the same red wine (Limnio) Odysseus used to get the cyclops Polyphemus drunk before blinding him with a spear. Just be sure to stay away from sharp objects.

Barley

Hordeum vulgare

Demeter was the goddess of the harvest, the mother of Persephone, and the giver of all grain. She may also have been the inventor of horchata. Modern horchata, often made with barley, is associated with Spanish-speaking cultures, but the word *horchata* is derived from the Latin word for barley: *hordeum*.

In ancient Greece the barley-based beverage was called a *kykeon*, which means a mixed drink. Some kykeons were wine based, but Demeter's kykeon was barley based. This kykeon was not only a refreshing beverage, it could also be a mighty intoxicant. And the kykeon was an essential part of the Eleusinian Mysteries, the celebration of Persephone's return to earth (*see* "Narcissus").

The Eleusinian Mysteries took place in the town of Eleusis, which is where Demeter stopped as she searched for her daughter, who had been abducted by Hades. While in Eleusis, Demeter, disguised as an old woman, agreed to care for the king's child. The child's mother offered Demeter a glass of wine, which Demeter refused. It was improper for her to drink wine since she was in mourning for her daughter. Instead, she asked for a special kykeon made from water, barley, and pennyroyal.

While that may not sound appetizing initially, remember that today horchata is a refreshing beverage made from either barley, rice, seeds, or chufa tubers, combined with water and sometimes also herbs and spices.

The Eleusinian Mysteries were a festival open to all Greeks except murderers and barbarians (the ancient Greeks labeled anyone who didn't speak their language a barbarian). For nine days in the fall, thousands of people celebrated the reunion of Demeter and Persephone and the beginning of the growing season. The Mysteries were sometimes described as orgiastic, but revealing the details of the ceremonies was a capital offense so we have very few specifics about what went on at Eleusis.

We *do* know that the ancient Greeks weren't kidding about keeping the Mysteries mysterious. In 415 BCE a huge political scandal swept Athens involving the mutilation of the herms (stones sacred to Hermes, carved with faces and phalluses) and the profanation of the Mysteries. Private citizens were accused of reenacting the Mysteries in their own homes, dressing up as priests, and perhaps even serving the kykeon. It is not hard to imagine a group of men, intoxicated from drinking kykeon, going out and raising hell with the herms. If this was indeed something resembling a fraternity prank, it did not go as planned. Executions ensued.

While the profanation of the Mysteries was well documented, the contents of the kykeon were not. Historians agree that the kykeon was an essential part of the ceremonies, consumed after three days of fasting and a night of dancing. And because the Mysteries have so often been described as ecstatic, many historians believe a hallucinogenic substance was included in the recipe along with the barley, water, and pennyroyal.

Perhaps a psychoactive ingredient *did* bring participants in the Mysteries to a state of ecstasy. They reported feeling one with the gods and believed their souls were immortal. Death was merely a temporary stage in the cycle of life, something to pass through, not something to be feared. Like Persephone, they would die and be reborn. It's also possible that after three days of fasting and dancing all night (basically an ancient rave) people were already in a state of altered consciousness.

Nevertheless, it's not unreasonable to suggest that a drug was involved. While some scholars believe opium may have been an ingredient in the kykeon, it would have been difficult to provide enough opium for the thousands of participants that came to Eleusis every year. The most common poppy in Greece was the corn poppy (*Papaver rhoeas*), which has no psychoactive properties.

Ergot, however, is a strong candidate for the kykeon intoxicant. It grows on more than three hundred different species of grass (grains are in the grass family) including barley and has a fascinating history. Ergot poisoning killed tens of thousands during the Middle Ages in Europe and is believed to have been partially responsible for the Salem witch trials. Consuming grain infected with ergot can cause hallucinations as well as the physical tremors and trances that make people appear possessed. While ergot does have a medicinal history (as both an abortifacient and to bring on childbirth), the dosage can be difficult to calculate since different species of ergot contain different levels of alkaloids. Long-term ergot poisoning can produce hallucinations, convulsions, and painful death.

Ergotamine, a chemical found in ergot, is currently used in very small doses to treat migraines and cluster headaches, usually in combination with caffeine. It is also a precursor to the synthesis of LSD, which is used therapeutically today to help terminal patients cope with their fear of approaching death. The kykeon did something similar for the participants in the Mysteries. After the ceremony, participants reported accepting death as part of the cycle of life rather than a terrifying event.

Today, barley is most often used for making beer and animal feed, although some is grown for human consumption. Fortunately, ergot is no longer a common agricultural problem. There is no fungicide effective against it, but better cultural practices have been developed that reduce its occurrence.

So make yourself a batch of ancient horchata with some modern-day (ergot-free) barley. You may not become one with the gods, but it's important to stay hydrated.

Mandrake

Mandragora spp.

Rumors about the magical powers of mandrake root have circulated from the time of the ancient Greeks through today, when Harry Potter and his pals transplant screaming mandrake roots at Hogwarts. Lest you think this makes mandrake a fictional plant, think again! Mandrakes are real, although the efficacy of some of their purported uses may not be.

Historically, mandrake (*Mandragora* spp.) has been used medicinally, most importantly as an anesthetic. Aristotle says mandrake is used to "induce sleep" and Plato describes it as a stupefying agent. Hippocrates suggests it for relieving suicidal thoughts, and Dioscorides lists dozens of applications for mandrake, including using a cupful to anesthetize surgical patients, mixing twenty grains of mandrake juice with honey and water to expel phlegm (although he cautions too much will kill), using five grains as an abortifacient, and mixing mandrake with water to cure scrofulous tumors.

Theophrastus, too, describes mandrake as a multipurpose medicine, used to treat gout, sleeplessness, and bacterial infections of the skin. He details the generally accepted wisdom on how to harvest the powerful mandrake root, but not before telling us that "the following ideas may be considered far-fetched and irrelevant."

> *Thus it is said that one should draw three circles round mandrake with a sword, and cut it with one's face toward the west; and at the cutting of the second piece one should dance round the plant and say as many things as possible about the mysteries of love.*

The last phrase above connects mandrake with love potions, and indeed, Aphrodite was sometimes known as Mandragoritis—She of the Mandrake.

The association of mandrake with aphrodisiacs was further supported by the shape of the plant's thick taproot. The root is often divided into two parts that resemble human legs. Irregular bumps and protuberances on the root were interpreted as breasts and/or genitalia. The idea that mandrake root could be used to promote lust and fertility carried into the seventeenth century, when John Donne instructed readers to "get with child a mandrake root."

In addition to being an aphrodisiac, mandrake was a party drug in ancient Greece. Because the Greeks diluted their wine (*see* "Grape"), it was less intoxicating than what we drink today. Greeks added a variety of herbs to the wine bowl to increase the inebriation factor, and mandrake was one of those herbs. Modern recipes for mandrake wine recommend steeping slightly less than an ounce of the dried root in a bottle of wine. Proceed with caution!

Rumors circulated in ancient Greece that digging up mandrake root would kill the digger, and Dioscorides tells us that hungry dogs were tied to partially excavated roots, then lured to pull up the root by a piece of raw meat. At least they got a last meal. Modern scholars speculate that the stories of danger associated with harvesting mandrake were perpetuated to discourage wholesale foraging of this valuable plant.

There are several different origin myths for mandrake. When Jason went in search of the Golden Fleece, he won the heart and assistance of Medea, daughter of the fleece's owner. In the *Argonautica*, Apollonius of Rhodes describes how Medea used the Herb of Prometheus to make Jason impervious to fire and bronze. There may also have been a little bit of love potion in there.

> *It shot up first-born when the ravening eagle on the rugged flanks of Caucasus let drip to the earth the blood-like ichor of tortured Prometheus. And its flower appeared a cubit above ground in colour like the Corycian crocus, rising on twin stalks; but in the earth the root was like newly cut flesh. . . . And beneath, the dark earth shook and bellowed when the Titanian root was cut; and the son of Iapetus himself groaned, his soul distraught with pain.*

Some modern scholars believe the Herb of Prometheus to be mandrake, and Apollonius's description of the flower (crocus-colored) and root (fleshlike) do indeed match up. He also tells us that both the earth and Prometheus (Iapetus's son) groan when the root is cut. (Hello, Harry Potter!)

The two *Mandragora* species common to the Mediterranean today are *M. officinarum* and *M. autumnalis*. Both have thick taproots that may resemble the human form if you squint or have drunk a lot of mandrake-infused wine. Both also contain the alkaloids atropine, scopolamine, and hyoscyamine, among others (*see* "Flying Herbs"). While many horticultural and medical texts classify the mandrake as poisonous, really, it's all in the dosage. All three of those alkaloids are included in the modern pharmacopoeia and are prescribed for specific conditions. Recent studies of the ripe fruit of *M. autumnalis* have shown the plant to have great potential as an antibacterial, antimicrobial, antidiabetic, and antiobesity drug.

Mandrake is a beautiful plant, with large, deeply veined, crinkly foliage surrounding upright purple flowers. It's hardy to USDA Zone 6 and thrives in well-drained soil, full sun, and low humidity. So why isn't it a popular garden plant? Just because Circe may have used it to transform Odysseus's men into pigs (*see* "Moly") doesn't mean you have to be a witch to appreciate mandrake. Ask for it at your local garden center but leave your spell book at home.

Flying Herbs

In the second century CE, Apuleius wrote *The Golden Ass*, the only Roman novel to survive in complete form today. Despite being written in Latin the story takes place in Greece. The hero travels through Thessaly and becomes fascinated by witchcraft. While there, he witnesses a Thessalian witch by the name of Pamphile transform herself:

> *First Pamphile completely stripped herself; then she opened a chest and took out a number of small boxes. From one of these she removed the lid and scooped out some ointment, which she rubbed between her hands for a long time before smearing herself with it all over from head to foot. Then there was a long muttered address to the lamp during which she shook her arms with a fluttering motion. As they gently flapped up and down there appeared on them a soft fluff, then a growth of strong feathers; her nose hardened into a hooked beak, her feet contracted into talons—and Pamphile was an owl.*

Thessaly was famous for its witches. Located in central Greece, Thessaly was geographically isolated, surrounded by mountains, including Mount Olympus to the north and Mount Pelion to the west. This part of Greece was considered primitive and barbaric by the citizens of Athens. It was a place of magic, where Artemis hunted and Cheiron the centaur taught his charges (including Achilles, Herakles, and Theseus) how to cure diseases. Where Medea came to search for her magic herbs.

The Oxford Companion to Classical Civilization states, "Thessaly boasted an old tradition of witchcraft, the Thessalian witches being notorious for their specialty of 'drawing down the moon.'" In *Natural History*, Pliny the Elder refers to this practice and the magic of the "matrons of Thessaly." He says the mere word Thessalian suggests witchcraft. And in Aristophanes's *Clouds*, reference is made to "those witchwomen from Thessaly." For this reference to have been effective, the theatergoing audience must have been familiar with the character of the Thessalian witch.

Scholars disagree as to whether the practice of "drawing down the moon" referred to predicting eclipses, or to pageantry performed with smoke, mirrors, and cloud cover. Either way, it was considered a specialty of the Thessalian witch and made for a convincing demonstration of power. In Apollonius of Rhodes's *Argonautica*, the moon herself accuses Medea of hiding the moon, so Medea can accomplish her witchcraft in darkness.

Medea arrived in Thessaly after fleeing her homeland of Colchis with Jason, who had (with her help) retrieved the Golden Fleece. She was a priestess of Hekate (goddess of witchcraft), and Apollonius tells us how she dug for magical herbs and how those herbs worked. Ovid says Medea flew in a chariot pulled by dragons as she searched for herbs on Mount Pelion, Mount Olympus, and in the Vale of Tempe (*see* "Laurel"). Mount Pelion is where Cheiron the centaur gathered his healing and magic herbs, and Theophrastus says the most productive drugs in Hellas come from Pelion in Thessaly. Both Mount Olympus and Mount Pelion are still known today for their variety of plant life.

Medea may have had a chariot pulled by dragons, but some witches, such as Pamphile, required the assistance of certain herbs in order to fly. It wasn't until the Middle Ages that the idea of flying broomsticks entered the picture, but millennia earlier, a set of herbs in the nightshade family (tomatoes/eggplants/peppers) was known to give the user the feeling of flying and transformation. These herbs later came to be called the flying herbs; they include deadly nightshade (*Atropa belladonna*), henbane (*Hyoscyamus* spp.), aconite (*Aconitum* spp.), and mandrake (*Mandragora* spp.).

Atropa belladonna is named after Atropos, the Fate who determined how long everyone would live, and who cut the cord of life when it was time to go. Some botanists speculate that *Atropa belladonna* was added to wine at Dionysian ceremonies, and Dioscorides recommends it as a sedative, although he warns that too much will make a patient faint. The primary active chemical in deadly nightshade is the alkaloid atropine, which is indeed a sedative. It may also cause disorientation and short-term memory loss. Atropine is used today in anesthesia for its ability to slow breathing and heart rate. It also lessens the toxic effect of aconitine (*see* "Aconite").

Aconite

Henbane

Nightshade

Yellow and black henbane (*H. albus*, *H. niger*) are both native to the Mediterranean. Dioscorides recommends them for "inflated genitals" (!?), although he cautions that boiled and eaten, a plateful will bring on a "mean disturbance of the senses." Henbane contains a high concentration of the alkaloid scopolamine, which can cause loss of muscle control, delirium, and intense hallucinations. Scopolamine is easily transferred through the skin to the blood stream. It also crosses the blood-brain barrier to act on the central nervous system. Today scopolamine is used in highly controlled doses, primarily to prevent motion sickness.

Robert Graves, author of *The Greek Myths*, reports that aconite was used by Thessalian witches in their flying ointments, saying it numbed their hands and feet. Not being able to feel the ground created a feeling of flying. Aconite has also been recorded as causing the body to feel covered in fur or feathers, and Ovid tells of Scythian women who used a magic potion to grow feathers all over their bodies. Was aconite an ingredient in this potion, creating a feathered feeling? While aconite doesn't possess psychoactive properties, it slows the heartbeat. This, combined with the feeling of numbness and the sensation of the body being covered with feathers, may well have made someone feel dizzy and as if they were flying.

Mandrake has been used as an anesthesia, a sedative, and a stupefying agent for thousands of years (*see* "Mandrake"). Like henbane and deadly nightshade, it contains the alkaloids scopolamine, atropine, and hyoscyamine.

These four plants have a psychotropic effect on the central nervous system, and all were well-known to physicians and herbalists in ancient Greece. It is entirely possible that those under the influence, whether the witches themselves or their audiences, might have believed they were flying, or hallucinated that they had been transformed into a nonhuman being.

None of these plants are common in today's gardens, although *Aconitum* species certainly should be. They are tall, strikingly gorgeous plants that bring vibrant color to the garden, even in shade. Some sources warn that the plants are toxic to touch, but there are no confirmed cases of aconite poisoning from everyday gardening. If this worries you, wear gloves.

In ancient Greece the term *witch* was used to condemn and isolate wise women and herbalists who were feared by those who didn't understand their talents. But knowing how to use herbs wasn't a bad thing, especially when the nascent medical establishment recommended cures like ground cockroaches in oil for earache, or poultices of greasy hair and fruit for pinworm.

Ostracizing witches has always been a way to manipulate the population through fear, and unfortunately, women were frequently the victims. But female herbalists were often the only understanding, sympathetic practitioners that women in ancient Greece had to rely on. Today Medea is portrayed as the ur-witch: evil, dangerous, and cruel, but as a woman in ancient Greece, she didn't have a lot of options. She was also intelligent, skilled, and made the best of her situation (cursed by Aphrodite, abandoned by her unfaithful husband, limited by the patriarchy). It's a wonder she didn't just fly away and leave the haters behind.

Cannabis

Cannabis spp.

The ancient Greeks were well versed in the intoxicating effects of cannabis, and while they were more inclined to party with wine than with weed, they appreciated cannabis in several ways: It was a well-known medicinal herb, cloth was woven from hemp fiber, and cannabis was used as a psychoactive substance in religious ceremonies.

There are several detailed accounts of cannabis use in ancient Greek texts. In *The History* (around 425 BCE), Herodotus describes a Scythian purification ritual.

> *They set up three sticks, leaning them against one another, and stretch, over these, woolen mats; and, having barricaded off this place as best they can, they make a pit in the center of the sticks and the mats and into it throw red-hot stones. . . .*

> *The Scythians take the seed of this hemp and, creeping under the mats, throw the seeds onto the stones as they glow with heat. The seed so cast on the stones gives off smoke and a vapor, no Greek steam bath could be stronger. The Scythians in their delight at the steam bath howl loudly.*

The Scythians were a nomadic people, famous for their horsemanship and fierce warriors. They settled across the Caucasus mountains and around the Black Sea and had established trading relationships with Greek colonies by the seventh century BCE. Archaeological evidence of the Scythian style of cannabis use was discovered in Ukraine in 1999, supporting Herodotus's description.

Perhaps cannabis was especially valued in warrior cultures as a way to take the edge off after a hard day on the battlefield. The Thracians were another group of fierce horsemen who probably used cannabis ceremonially. They inhabited land that today is part of Bulgaria, Romania, Greece, and Turkey. Certain Thracian shamans were known as *kapnobatai* (smoke-walkers), and some modern scholars believe the smoke referenced in their ceremonies was cannabis smoke, used to induce ecstasy and oracular visions.

Speaking of oracles, the Oracle of the Dead was located in Ephyra on the banks of the Acheron River. This was in northern Greece (not far from Thrace) and was considered one of the entrances to Hades. Ancient Greeks would spend weeks there preparing to speak with their ancestors, participating in cleansing rituals, and eating special foods that may also have contained a psychoactive compound. Archaeologists have discovered lumps of hash (a potent paste made from the resin of female cannabis plants) at Ephyra, leading them to speculate that as the faithful slept at the temple, hash may have been burned as incense or used to promote vivid dreams or communication with the dearly departed.

Modern botanists disagree on how many species of cannabis exist, but most recreational and medicinal cannabis strains are considered to belong to *C. sativa* and *C. indica*. Archaeological evidence shows that the Scythians used *C. ruderalis*, a shorter, more cold-hardy species of cannabis, native to Siberia. It is lower in THC than our modern cannabis cultivars but contains more CBD. This is an auto-flowering plant, which blooms at maturity rather than in response to daylight hours. It generally reaches the flowering stage in about ten weeks. This was a useful characteristic in the colder climates around the Black Sea, allowing multiple harvests in a single season. (*C. sativa* and *C. indica* require three to eight months from seed to harvest.) Today *C. ruderalis* is used in hybridization to create auto-flowering plants with higher CBD levels, improved cold hardiness, and shorter height.

C. sativa was included in the *United States Pharmacopoeia* (USP) until 1942, recommended as a mild sedative, and generally accepted by physicians as helpful, not harmful. But in the 1930s, Harry J. Anslinger, head of the Federal Bureau of Narcotics, waged war on weed. The internet is full of outrageous, racist quotes attributed to Anslinger, but few are from primary sources. What is substantiated, however, is that Anslinger ignored a report from the American Medical Association that objected to the proposal to ban cannabis as a legitimate medicine. Nor did he hesitate to regale politicians and the press with lurid (and often unsubstantiated) stories of cannabis-fueled murder.

Modern researchers disagree as to whether Anslinger's objections to cannabis were based on racism or on the fact that disappointed prohibitionists (of which he was one) needed a new demon to focus on once prohibition was repealed. Anslinger manipulated facts and played upon anti-Black and anti-Mexican sentiment by insinuating that cannabis was peddled by "hot tamale" vendors and was essential to musicians playing jazz and swing, i.e., people of color. His sensationalist propaganda led to the making of the movie *Reefer Madness* (1936), which was intended as a cautionary tale but is actually hilariously cartoonish.

The result of this sensationalist and biased publicity was the Marijuana Tax Act (1937) and the removal of cannabis from the USP (1942). But you can't keep a good herb down! The tax act was repealed in 1969, and today medicinal marijuana is legal in thirty-eight states. Recreational use is currently legal in twenty-four, which means that in those states cannabis can be cultivated as a garden plant. Currently, federal law classifies cannabis as a Schedule I substance under the Controlled Substances Act along with heroin, making its use more restricted than fentanyl, hydrocodone, and oxycodone. But the US DEA has recently proposed moving it to Schedule III, thus acknowledging its usefulness as a medicine.

As cannabis becomes legal across the United States, more people are growing it at home, not only for its medicinal and recreational benefits but because it's a great-looking plant! Cannabis is an annual and is also dioecious, meaning male and female flowers form on separate plants. Those who want to grow cannabis for consumption grow only female plants. Those who appreciate it as a large, lush garden plant with gorgeous foliage may not care about the sex of the plant, although female flowers are larger and more attractive than male flowers.

Cannabis grows best in full sun and well-drained soils. Despite the fact that its flowers have no petals, both the blooms and foliage can be highly ornamental, especially in fall as the flowers ripen and foliage of some varieties take on reddish-purple colors. Cannabis grows well both in the ground and in containers. While some strains can grow to be twelve feet tall, growing the plant in a container will limit its mature size.

Cannabis is finally becoming accepted around the world as both a medicinal and recreational herb. Now we can all celebrate like the Scythians.

Opium Poppy

Papaver somniferum

I n ancient Greece the poppy was more than a beautiful flower or the source of a bagel topping. It was a valued medicine, an important anesthetic, and the floral reincarnation of Demeter's mortal lover.

It wasn't only the male gods who fraternized with humans. Demeter, goddess of the harvest, had a mortal lover named Mekon. She transformed him into a poppy to preserve his beauty after he died, and the poppy plant was henceforth called *mekon*. That's it. No trickery, no abduction, no drama. Mekon was a handsome young man. He and Demeter were lovers. She turned him into a poppy. The end. And while it's frustrating not to have more details (at least none that have been preserved through the ages), it's also kind of nice to hear a simple love story for a change. Today the genus *Meconopsis* is part of the poppy family, and includes the rare and wonderful blue poppy.

Demeter is also associated with the poppy because of its medicinal properties. As she wandered the earth searching for her daughter Persephone (*see* "Narcissus") she was so distraught she could not sleep. It was only by consuming the poppy that she could find relief. In *Fasti*, Ovid tells us, "she plucked a tender, sleep-inducing poppy from the bare ground."

The narcotic and medicinal properties of the opium poppy were well-known in ancient times, and the poppy had reached Greece by the middle of the second millennium BCE. Paintings, statues, and jewelry clearly show poppy capsules as valuable, sacred objects. One of the most interesting ancient Greek artifacts is a statue of a Minoan goddess discovered on Crete that dates to somewhere between 1400–1100 BCE. Three poppy capsules (seed heads) decorate her crown and the capsules show notching lines, made to extract the juice from the capsules. Her eyes are closed and her mouth is gently smiling. Is she under the influence of opium?

In the *Odyssey*, Homer describes a drug called *nepenthe*, which some scholars speculate may have been opium. After the Trojan War was over, Odysseus struggled for ten years to return home. His wife Penelope and his son Telemachus didn't know whether he was dead or alive. Penelope sent Telemachus to Sparta to ask Menelaus and Helen if they had news of Odysseus. As Telemachus and Menelaus talked, they wept for their lost friends and family. To relieve their pain, Helen added a drug to their wine. The ancient Greek word for that drug is *nepenthe*, which translates literally to "antisorrow." Homer tells us that nepenthe dissolved anger and made pain disappear. "No one who drank it deeply, mulled in wine, could let a tear roll down his cheeks that day, not even if his mother should die, his father die."

The plants we call *Nepenthes* today have no such properties. They are primarily tropical pitcher plants native to the South Pacific that trap insects and small lizards in their pitchers, then digest them. Carl Linnaeus named the plant after the mythological drug because he thought it was such a wonder it would make botanists forget all "past ills." While it is certainly a very cool plant, its ability to distract from all past ills is highly overrated.

Some scholars believe the nepenthe of the *Odyssey* may have been opium, but others suspect it was cannabis or henbane. However, all three of these plants were known and used medicinally in ancient Greece before the time of Homer, so why wouldn't he specify which of these was nepenthe? Theophrastus also knew these plants and described their uses in his writing, extolling their medicinal and practical virtues. Yet he refers to the properties of nepenthe as hearsay, telling us that Homer says "it causes forgetfulness and indifference to ills." Still, as opium did for Demeter, so did nepenthe do for Telemachus and Menelaus. Their grief melted away and they were relieved, both mentally and physically.

A quick review of ancient Greek medicines reveals that very few were "simples," i.e., medicines composed of a single ingredient. Many were complicated compositions, combining long lists of ingredients. For example, Hippocrates offers the following prescription to relieve a type of consumption: "parsley root, dill, rue, mint, coriander, fresh poppy, basil, lentils, sweet pomegranate juice, and pomegranate vinegar." Most likely Helen's nepenthe was a combination of opium with other narcotic and psychoactive plants, which she added to wine.

The opium poppy is a gorgeous plant, much loved for its rich, colorful blooms. It is also considered a Schedule II controlled substance by

the DEA. Depending on whom you ask, it either is or isn't illegal to grow opium poppies in the United States. It is *definitely* illegal to grow them with the intent to make drugs. Since this is the same poppy from which we get poppy seeds (which were used in bread-making in ancient Greece just as they are today), the DEA would have to prove you were growing them as a drug rather than as a spice or for their beauty. In an effort to mollify (or deceive) law enforcement, these plants are sometimes sold as "seed" poppies.

In addition to bakers and gardeners, florists also suffer from the DEA's prohibition against opium poppies. Dried poppy seed capsules are highly ornamental and have long been used in floral arrangements. While opium poppy seeds contain mere traces of morphine and are legal to possess and consume, the dried plant is not. It is considered "poppy straw" and can be used to make a soporific tea that is described as having much the same effect as Demeter's poppy and Helen's nepenthe: pain relief with a sense of euphoria. The possession of poppy straw is now illegal and as a result many wholesale flower sellers no longer sell the decorative dried capsules of opium poppies.

As Michael Pollan wrote in *This Is Your Mind on Plants*, the legality of poppy growing is difficult to decipher. While the DEA may tell you it's entirely illegal, several courts have dismissed cases where criminal intent could not be proved. In other words, if you're a gardener with a few poppies in your garden, you're probably ok. But if that same gardener shares a recipe for making a soporific tea from poppy straw . . . not so much.

IT'S ALL IN
THE DOSAGE

Yarrow

Aconite

Poison Hemlock

Dittany

Medicinal Herbs

Pennyroyal

Yarrow

Achillea millefolium

"Sing, goddess, of the rage of Achilles."

Thus begins the *Iliad*, an epic poem known more for its bloody descriptions of battles than for its appreciation of horticulture. But while Achilles is well-known as ancient Greece's fiercest warrior, few people realize he was schooled in herbalism by the centaur Cheiron. One plant in particular remains associated with Achilles even today. The yarrow plant, *Achillea millefolium*, is named for Achilles, and mythology tells us he used it to heal his men on the battlefield.

Achilles was the son of Thetis, a sea nymph, and Peleus, a mortal. Zeus had his eye on the lovely Thetis, but when Prometheus told Zeus that Thetis was fated to bear a son more powerful than his father, Zeus decided he could live without her. In fact, this information was the bargaining chip that convinced Zeus to release Prometheus from his millennia of torture (*see* "Fennel").

The myth of Achilles's heel is a familiar one. Thetis dipped him in the river Styx to make him invulnerable, holding him just above the heel, thereby leaving that one spot unprotected—which eventually led to his downfall. But the myth of the Styx-dipping appeared much later than

Homer's *Iliad*, in an epic poem known as the *Achilleid*, written by the Roman poet Statius. In the *Iliad*, Achilles is neither immortal nor invulnerable. He's a superb warrior, but he can be and is wounded in battle, albeit not fatally.

Pre-Homeric stories describe how Thetis tried to protect her son by burning away his mortality in fire or boiling it away in water. She was interrupted by Peleus, who believed she was killing their child. Because Thetis was interrupted, her magic did not work, and Achilles remained mortal.

In anger, Thetis returned to the sea, leaving Peleus as a single dad. That wasn't really a man's job in ancient Greece, so Peleus sent his son to be raised and educated by Cheiron the centaur. Centaurs had the upper body of a human and the legs of a horse, and most were licentious lawbreakers. But Cheiron was an intellectual, responsible for the education of heroes and demigods like Herakles, Theseus, and Achilles. He taught Achilles how to fight, hunt, and make music. He also taught him about medicine, which came in handy on the battlefield. In turn, Achilles taught these skills to his companion, Patroclus. When Eurypylus was wounded at Troy, he asked Patroclus to "spread the soothing, healing salves across it, / the powerful drugs they say you learned from Achilles / and Chiron the most humane of Centaurs taught your friend."

In fact, yarrow *does* contain a blood-clotting agent and has been used as such for millennia around the globe. Yarrow pollen has been found at Neanderthal sites (dating back more than sixty thousand years), and DNA analysis has recently identified yarrow as a medicinal herb recovered from a Roman ship in the second century BCE. The alkaloid achilleine is actively styptic, meaning it stops the flow of blood. This is useful if you scrape a knee on the trail, or perhaps if you're nicked by an arrow on the battlefield. It does not help if you're pierced through the chest by a spear.

An injury to the lower leg is not usually fatal, and since the myth of Achilles's heel was not recorded until almost a millennium after the Trojan War, let's entertain another theory, one that supports the idea

that Achilles was not originally perceived to be either invulnerable or immortal. Ancient artwork often shows Achilles shot in the lower leg, close to the heel, but at least one painting shows a second arrow piercing the body of Achilles in the chest and others show Paris (whose relationship with Helen of Troy started the whole kerfuffle) preparing to shoot a second arrow. Jonathan Burgess, a classics professor at the University of Toronto, suggests that the arrow to the leg immobilized Achilles, who was known for being extraordinarily fleet of foot. Once Achilles could no longer move, a second arrow, aimed at a more essential body part, dealt the mortal blow. For that kind of wound, yarrow would be no use at all.

In his *Natural History*, Pliny says that Achilles discovered a healing plant thereafter named for him as *achilleos*. Pliny offers descriptions of several possible plant candidates, one of which matches up with the yarrow we know today. He calls the plant *millefolium* and describes it as having a stem about one and a half feet tall with leaves smaller than those of fennel. Like fennel, yarrow does indeed have finely dissected, feathery leaves. Its flower stem grows to be approximately one and a half feet tall.

Many European countries including Germany, France, and Switzerland list yarrow in their modern pharmacopoeias, and research continues into its antioxidant, antibacterial, anti-inflammatory, and anti-fungal properties. Currently, it is primarily used as an herbal treatment for wound healing and gastrointestinal disorders.

Gardeners appreciate yarrow as a full-sun, drought-tolerant garden perennial. Modern hybrids offer flowers in red, yellow, pink, and orange, in addition to the white flowers of the straight species. It attracts pollinators and beneficial insects to the garden, and its soft, feathery foliage makes an effective groundcover for a sunny border.

Yarrow is also an interesting and underappreciated herb, with a flavor similar to anise and tarragon, albeit with a bitter finish. Its roots have a more intense flavor and can be used as the base for homemade cocktail bitters. Admittedly, yarrow has an aggressive growth habit, but if you find yourself with too much in the garden, dig some up and make yourself a drink.

Aconite

Aconitum spp.

Such a beautiful flower. Such a dangerous plant. In antiquity, aconite was used as a poison on wild animals, uncooperative spouses, soldiers, threats to the monarchy, or anyone else who needed killing. Its alternate names—queen of poisons, wolfsbane, woman-killer, and devil's helmet—make its power as a poison perfectly clear.

This plant was sacred to Hekate, goddess of witchcraft, who is sometimes credited with its invention. Other stories suggest that aconite sprang from the blood of Prometheus as he was tortured, but most often mythology attributes the creation of aconite to Herakles and Kerberos (sometimes spelled Cerberus), the three-headed guard dog of the underworld.

For his twelfth labor, Herakles was tasked with bringing Kerberos up to the earth's surface. Hades gave him permission to try, if he could do so without using any weapons. Not surprisingly (except perhaps to Hades), Herakles accomplished this with nothing more than his bare hands. Kerberos was not used to the bright light of day and became ill when exposed to the sun. He threw up, and his vomit landed on the ground, giving birth to the aconite plant. No need to call PETA! Kerberos was returned to the underworld once Herakles got credit for the labor.

Aconite was sacred to the goddess Hekate, and Medea was a priestess of Hekate. Medea fell in love with Jason and helped him steal the Golden Fleece from her father. After being abandoned by Jason (and killing their children in revenge), she married Aegeus, king of Athens, and together they had a son named Medus. Aegeus, however, already had a son, Theseus. Aegeus had placed his sword and sandals under a giant rock before leaving Theseus's mother to raise the boy on her own. Aegeus said that if one day Theseus were heroic enough to move the rock, he should bring the sword and sandals to Athens to claim his birthright.

When Theseus arrived in Athens, his father didn't recognize him although Medea knew exactly who he was. She had no intention of allowing Theseus to usurp Medus's right to the throne, and made Aegeus suspicious of the newcomer. With Aegeus's permission, she added aconite to Theseus's wine cup. But just as Theseus raised the cup to his lips Aegeus recognized the emblem of his own royal house on Theseus's sword and knocked the poisoned beverage from Theseus's hand. Medea left town on the next stagecoach.

In *Metamorphoses*, Ovid tells how the goddess Athena punished the mortal girl Arachne for daring to compare her skill as a weaver to that of Athena. Athena sprinkled Arachne with the juice of Hekate's herb and turned her into a spider, forced to weave forever. (Get it? Arachne . . . arachnid . . . spiders are known to taxonomists as *arachnids*.) While there are other herbs considered sacred to Hekate, classical scholars agree the herb in question was aconite.

Also in *Metamorphoses*, Ovid tells the story of King Athamas of Thebes and his wife, Ino, one of Dionysus's aunts. Hera hated Dionysus and everyone associated with him. She never forgave Zeus for his affair with Semele, Dionysus's mortal mother (*see* "Grape"), and was determined to punish Ino, simply because Ino was Semele's sister. Hera descended to Hades where she enlisted the help of the Furies. They composed a potion that included the "slaver from Cerberus" (aconite) and poured it onto King Athamas and Ino. "It scorched their inmost vitals" and their minds were "stricken with wild rage."

Theophrastus, the father of botany, describes the plant in detail but claims that it is difficult to use effectively and that very few physicians understand how to use it correctly. He tells us that possession of the plant was punishable by death. Centuries later, aconite was still a plant to be feared. Pliny the Elder wrote that touching a single leaf of aconite to the genitals of a female mammal would kill the animal within a day. He also claimed that the Roman politician Lucius Calpurnius Bestia killed three of his wives this way, although history views this as a purely political accusation. And lest you credit Pliny with too much wisdom, he also stated that the antidote to aconite poisoning was eating human feces. So there's that.

Aconite has been used to poison arrows for millennia, and some claim the arrow that pierced Achilles's heel was dipped in aconite, transforming a minor wound into a fatal blow. In *Alexipharmaca*—a poem about poisons and their antidotes—Nicander of Colophon describes how aconite poison works. First the victim experiences a crushing, choking feeling, which is followed by intense stomach pain. Next the temples throb rapidly and the victim sees double. It's a painful way to go.

Today *Aconitum napellus* is valued both for its finely cut foliage and its gorgeous, purple-blue flowers which are borne in tall flower spikes. This is an exceptional perennial, a gorgeous garden plant. Its unusual bloom shape resembles that of a monk's cowl, hence its least malevolent common name: monkshood. This plant grows best in cool climates, moist well-drained soils, and sun to part shade. It is almost never bothered by pests, who somehow intuit that monkshood is not good food.

The toxic component in aconite is aconitine, which can cause fatal arrythmias. The toxicity of aconitine is said to be reduced by boiling, and the plant is used in some traditional medicines. In Chinese medicine the roots are used to treat rheumatic fever, diarrhea, and joint pain, among other ailments. In India, the plant has been used to combat fever and inflammation, after being boiled in cow's urine for two days. In Western medicine it is generally considered unsafe.

Rumors of monkshood being poisonous to touch persist today, but they are false. The plant is only toxic when consumed, something that President Sadyr Japarov of Kyrgyzstan was apparently unaware of when he recommended an infusion of aconite root as treatment for COVID-19. The country's health minister, Alymkadyr Beishenaliev, sipped some on camera, warning that it was only safe to drink when consumed hot. My guess is he was drinking ordinary tea, because four people were rushed to the hospital after consuming the toxic beverage following the broadcast.

Poison Hemlock

Conium maculatum

Almost everyone has heard the story of the death of Socrates, executed in 399 BCE with a draught of poison hemlock. Socrates had been found guilty of impiety and corrupting the youth of Athens and was sentenced to death. He was given the opportunity to flee the city and save his own life, but he refused. The man knew how to make an exit.

Poison hemlock is an entirely different plant from the popular evergreen hemlock tree in the genus *Tsuga*. Poison hemlock grew throughout Greece and still does today. It also grows in forty-six of the fifty US states and five Canadian provinces. It's an attractive plant with a pretty white flower, an aggressive growth habit, and a strong resemblance to Queen Anne's lace, aka the safe-to-eat wild carrot.

In Plato's *Phaedo*, we watch Socrates as the poison takes effect. It doesn't seem like a bad way to go. Socrates remains clear-headed, not in pain. He gets tired, lies down, and eventually stops breathing. But was it really hemlock that killed Socrates? Plato uses the word *pharmakon*, which translates simply as "drug." The drug is not named specifically in any contemporaneous text, and researchers have relied on the description of Socrates's death to make their best guess at which plant did the deed.

Plato wrote the *Phaedo* circa 360 BCE, about forty years after the death of Socrates. He was not actually present at the death, and forty years was plenty of time for details to have faded from memory. Socrates is described as drinking the poison, walking and talking until his legs felt heavy, then lying down, still able to converse until he quietly took his last breath. But some classical scholars suggest that Plato may have tinkered with the death scene to give Socrates dignity.

Even today there is no antidote for hemlock poisoning, although Nicander suggests administering wine, pepper, nettle seeds, grape syrup, or foaming milk. Approximately two hundred years after Socrates's death, Nicander describes hemlock as having drastically more painful effects than those described by Plato.

> *This drink assuredly looses disaster upon the head, bringing the darkness of night: the eyes roll, and men roam the streets with tottering steps and crawling upon their hands; a terrible choking blocks the lower throat and the narrow passage of the windpipe; the extremities grow cold; and in the limbs the stout arteries are contracted; for a short while the victim draws breath like one swooning, and his spirit beholds Hades.*

Why are these two descriptions of hemlock poisoning so different? Neither Plato nor Nicander were botanists or doctors, so let's consult the professionals.

In the first century CE, Dioscorides wrote that hemlock is venomous and can kill, but he also suggested several topical applications and recommended smearing the pounded plant onto testicles to curb lustful dreams and nocturnal emissions. Just a few years later, Pliny the Elder

referred to hemlock used in Athens for capital punishment. He also offered several topical applications for the plant, but says only the seed is poisonous, and that the stem can be eaten. **Safety Alert: This is not true! Do not eat poison hemlock!**

Theophrastus provides some insight. He mentions that in general, people become more skilled at making medicines and poisons over time. He uses the people of Keos as an example, saying that in the past they merely shredded their hemlock but now they peel it, bruise it, and make a drink from it, and that *this* brings a swift and easy death.

What's this about the people of Keos? Why were they considered experts on hemlock? Theophrastus is referring to the story about the island of Keos in which elderly citizens who were no longer able to contribute to society committed suicide by drinking hemlock. Menander, a contemporary of Theophrastus, describes the "fine custom" of the Keians: "that a man who can't live well does not continue to live ill." Obviously, if the Keian government expected its people to comply with the suicide directive, it would help if the death were swift and easy, rather than painful, choking, and spasmodic, as described by Nicander.

Which brings us back to why we have two such different descriptions of hemlock poisoning. Perhaps Nicander and Plato were describing poisoning symptoms from two different plants. In the nineteenth century, a group of physicians and toxicologists performed well-documented research, administering poison hemlock to their patients (yes, really) and to themselves in an effort to determine its medicinal properties. The results of their experiments matched Plato's description of a quiet death, one achieved by affecting the peripheral nervous system, i.e., all nerves outside the brain and spinal cord.

So which plant caused the violent reactions that Nicander wrote about? Water hemlock (*Cicuta maculata*) causes symptoms that match up well with Nicander's description: vomiting, diarrhea, seizures, and cardiac arrest. These results are what we expect from a poison working on the central nervous system, i.e., the brain and the spinal cord.

It's not difficult to understand where the confusion came from. The names for poison hemlock and water hemlock were used interchangeably until Linnaeus came up with his binomial system of plant nomenclature in the mid-eighteenth century. The plants look superficially alike, with umbels of delicate white flowers and finely cut foliage. They are both members of the carrot family, and both can be deadly, although their effects on the human body are quite different.

Poison hemlock contains multiple alkaloids that act as poisons, resulting in weakness, difficulty breathing, and paralysis. Interestingly, environmental conditions can affect the potency of these alkaloids; hot and dry growing conditions (like those in Greece) produce higher concentrations of the alkaloids. The difference between toxic and therapeutic doses is very slim, however, and poison hemlock is rarely used in modern medicine. Current studies of poison hemlock as an anticancer drug are promising, but until more research is complete, better to admire from a distance.

Dittany

Origanum dictamnus

Dittany is a species of oregano native exclusively to the island of Crete. For millennia this rare and valued plant grew only in deep gorges and the crevices of cliffs, making it perilous to harvest. Some classicists believe the plant was named after Mount Dikte on Crete, one of two possible birthplaces of Zeus. Others suggest it was named for Diktynna, a virgin hunting goddess of Crete, whose cult eventually merged with that of Artemis. Either way, dittany was believed to have magical as well as medicinal properties.

When Aeneas was wounded during the Trojan War, the shaft of the arrow that struck him broke off, leaving the arrowhead embedded in his thigh. His physician tried cutting out the arrowhead, but could not budge it until Aeneas's mother, Aphrodite, brought dittany to heal the wound. Virgil describes the plant as having "downy leaves and scarlet flower, a plant that wild goats know about when stuck with arrows." When the Trojan doctor bathed Aeneas's wound in water infused with dittany, "all anguish instantly left Aeneas's body, all his bleeding stopped, deep in the wound. The arrowhead came out."

Dittany is indeed a plant with woolly leaves and a pink flower, but what's this about goats stuck with arrows? In *History of Animals*, Aristotle says certain animals act intelligently; he illustrates this point: "Wild goats in Crete are said, when wounded by arrows, to go in search of dittany, which is supposed to have the property of ejecting arrows in the body." In ancient Greece, dittany was sometimes called *artemidion* in honor of Artemis, goddess of the hunt. It was considered a gift from her, sent to cure the wounds caused by arrows, which were her weapon of choice.

The ancient Greeks considered dittany to be a panacea and used it to treat dozens of different ailments and injuries. In *Diseases of Women*, Hippocrates recommends dittany for gastric upset, menstruation issues, and abortion. Dioscorides says it helps with snakebites, heals gangrenous ulcerations, and expels dead embryos. Theophrastus (who was a student of Aristotle) repeats the story of the goats, then adds some practical information about the herb. He recommends it for women in childbirth, saying that the leaves ease the pain and difficulty of labor.

Dittany has long been associated with reproductive health, including more than two thousand years of use as an emmenagogue—an herb that stimulates menstrual flow, which was believed to be important for several reasons. The ancient Greeks understood that regular menstruation was important for female health. They believed it purified the body, balanced the humors (blood, phlegm, yellow bile, and black bile), and rid the body of excess blood. But emmenagogues were—and sometimes still are—also used to bring on abortions: If a woman hasn't gotten her period because she's pregnant, bringing on her period terminates the pregnancy.

In *Moralia*, Plutarch doesn't beat around the bush. He repeats the old story about the arrows falling out of goats, then extrapolates from goats to pregnant women.

> *And Cretan goats, when they eat dittany, easily expel arrows from their bodies and so have presented an easy lesson for women with child to take to heart, that the herb has an abortive property; for there is nothing except dittany that the goats, when they are wounded, rush to search for.*

Making the leap from goats to pregnant women and from arrows to fetuses may have made for an interesting analogy in ancient Greece, but it is certainly not medically or physiologically accurate.

Modern scientific research into the antimicrobial, antioxidant, cytotoxic, and insecticidal properties of dittany have shown significant promise. Interestingly, it has proven especially effective in treating gastric ulcers, supporting Hippocrates's recommendation of dittany for stomach upset. There is currently no research being done into dittany's effectiveness as birth control.

Until the 1920s, dittany was harvested exclusively from the wild. As demand grew and native populations became threatened, Cretan farmers near Mount Dikte began to cultivate the herb. Today, wild dittany is classified as vulnerable by the International Union for Conservation of Nature and is also protected by a Greek presidential decree. Most of what is harvested is exported and used by distilleries as a popular vermouth ingredient. You'll find it in Cinzano Bianco and Martini Rosso. And while the makers of Bénédictine refuse to divulge their long list of flavorful herbs, dittany is believed to be one of its ingredients.

Modern gardeners value dittany more for its beauty than for its flavor, which is less strong than that of common oregano (*O. vulgare*). But what dittany lacks in flavor it more than makes up for with good looks. Its small, almost round leaves are held in opposite pairs and are entirely covered with white hairs, giving it a soft, fuzzy appearance. The actual flowers are small, but they are surrounded with layers of pink-purple ornamental bracts that resemble hops flowers in shape. This is an excellent plant for a rock garden or the top of a garden wall, where the pendant flower stems can hang gracefully over the edge.

Rumors of dittany's magical powers persist to this day. In *Harry Potter and the Deathly Hallows*, it's used twice, once to cure Ron Weasley after he was splinched (teleported unsuccessfully, leaving a few body parts behind), and once to heal Harry, Hermione, and Ron after they were injured raiding Bellatrix Lestrange's vault. The ancient Greeks might have agreed with J. K. Rowling that dittany has magical powers, but a modern Cretan *yiayia* would offer you dittany tea as a remedy for an upset stomach. As long as you're not pregnant.

Medicinal Herbs

I n the fifth century BCE, Hippocrates may (or may not) have famously said, "Let food be thy medicine and let thy medicine be food." While he could have merely been encouraging his fellow ancient Greeks to eat a healthy diet, Hippocrates knew that many herbs used to flavor food had important medicinal properties.

—— Mugwort ——

Artemisia vulgaris

Mugwort's botanical name comes from Artemis, virgin goddess of the hunt. She also protected pregnant women and was considered one of the goddesses of childbirth. If childbirth and virginity seem contradictory, just wait. Some authors claim that the Artemisia festivals began as orgiastic springtime celebrations held at the time of the full moon. These festivals included fertility rites and the ingestion of mugwort as a symbolic gesture of consuming the goddess.

Mugwort has long been valued as a medicinal herb, especially for treating gynecological issues. Its ability to bring on uterine contractions makes it useful both as an abortifacient and to assist with childbirth. When smoked, it is a mild intoxicant and relaxant, which would certainly help ease labor pains. Recent studies have shown that leaf extracts of mugwort have an estrogenic effect (which helps regulate the menstrual cycle) and a strong anti-implantation effect (which can prevent pregnancy).

Artemis was severe and unyielding; she had no sympathy for those who breached her rules of chastity and propriety. Just ask the hunter Actaeon, who accidentally saw Artemis bathing naked. His punishment: She turned him into a deer that was torn to pieces by his own hounds. But when it came to women suffering the pain of childbirth, Artemis was there to help in the form of her namesake herb.

—— Parsley ——

Petroselinum crispum

Nemea was a small city in the northern Peloponnese, and the royal family there had an infant son named Opheltes. When Opheltes was born, his father asked the oracle at Delphi how to ensure his child would have a long and happy life. The oracle told him the baby must not touch the ground until he had learned to walk.

One day, Opheltes's nurse Hypsipyle was distracted by soldiers who stopped to ask for water on their journey. Perhaps she hadn't heard the prophecy, because she placed Opheltes on a bed of celery on the ground. Hypsiplye gave the soldiers water and got to chatting, telling her life story of disappointed love, children born out of wedlock, and captivity leading to a life of slavery.

While the nurse was otherwise engaged, a serpent bit the young prince and killed him. The herb parsley grew from his blood. The silver lining? Funeral games were held in Opheltes's honor, and these became the Nemean Games, one of four Panhellenic Games, like the Olympics. Winners at the Nemean Games were crowned with a wreath of celery.

—— Rue ——

Ruta graveolens

King Mithridates was the ruler of Pontus, along the Black Sea in modern-day Turkey. Despite being known as a fierce and ruthless warrior he was terrified of being poisoned. (His father had been assassinated by poisoning.) So Mithridates developed what he believed was a universal antidote. Pliny the Elder reports that the recipe was found after Mithridates's death; the primary ingredient was the herb rue.

Equally interesting (and unlikely) is the story of how Medea threw rue into the ocean as she and Jason sailed past the island of Lemnos on their way back to Greece from Colchis, where they had stolen the Golden Fleece. Rue is known for its unpleasant-smelling foliage, and the story says that as the rue-strewn water reached the Lemnian women swimming in the sea, it made them smell so bad that no man would go near them. But why did Medea care about how the Lemnian women smelled?

Previously, when Jason and his crew were on their way to Colchis, they stopped on Lemnos. The women there had killed their husbands and they welcomed Jason and his crew with open arms and open beds. Jason fathered twin sons by the princess of Lemnos, and even though this was before Jason met Medea, she was jealous. She wasn't taking any chances on a repeat performance, hence the tossing of the rue. By delightful coincidence, the Lemnian princess who bore Jason's twins just happened to be Hypsipyle! (*See* "Parsley," above.)

Today, rue is known to be effective at preventing implantation of the embryo. It is also a well-known abortifacient and can cause infertility in male mammals. Perhaps Medea was onto something.

—— Tansy ——

Tanacetum vulgare

Ganymede was the son of Tros, for whom the city of Troy was named. Ganymede was said to be the most beautiful of mortals (according to Homer), and Zeus fell in love with him. While Ganymede was tending sheep, Zeus either sent an eagle down to bring the boy back to Mount Olympus or did the kidnapping himself in the form of an eagle. Ganymede was thereafter the cupbearer to Zeus; he mixed and poured the wine for the god. He may also have provided other personal services.

In Plato's *Laws*, one character speaks against homosexuality. He argues against the story of Ganymede as Zeus's special friend and claims the Cretans made up the story to give themselves permission to do as Zeus did and enjoy the company of young male lovers.

Zeus gave Ganymede's father a pair of the finest horses in compensation for stealing his son. These were the horses the gods themselves rode and Troy was thereafter famous for its horses. To Ganymede, Zeus gave a drink of tansy, which made the boy immortal. Despite its history as a medicinal herb, today tansy is considered toxic in some forms. The essential oils of tansy contain thujone, which is toxic to humans in high doses. Water-based extractions, including teas, have been used safely by herbalists for millennia. We don't know what kind of tansy-based beverage Zeus gave Ganymede, but it's possible he had to die, leaving his mortal life behind, before he could become immortal. Today Ganymede lives on in the sky as the constellation Aquarius, the water-bearer.

While many medicinal herbs used by the ancient Greeks are still considered effective, some ancient Greek remedies seem astonishingly ridiculous to the modern reader. (Who among us would agree to drink wine mixed with mule excrement?) Yet despite the fact that the ancient Greeks had no modern laboratories or equipment, they managed to understand enough to devise a few effective remedies that herbalists continue to use today.

Pennyroyal

Mentha pulegium

The Greeks liked sex and they weren't afraid to talk about it. Professional sex, underage sex, same-sex sex . . . you name it, they did it. The only kind of sex they feared was out-of-wedlock sex by the wives of Greek citizens, because that could endanger birthrights and inheritances and then all hell would break loose.

The wives of Greek citizens had one job: to bear legitimate children. They had no political power, no economic autonomy, no artistic outlets (Sappho was an exception). Since childbearing was women's primary duty, birth control was not a topic of much concern to the male medical establishment. Women had to look out for their own reproductive health, and in ancient Greece women were familiar with a range of plant-based contraceptives and abortifacients. Pennyroyal was among the most effective. It was also one of the most dangerous.

The widespread understanding of pennyroyal's contraceptive properties is confirmed by Theophrastus, Dioscorides, and Hippocrates. The information was so widely known that Aristophanes used it as a joke in his comedy *Peace*. In the play, Hermes gives the long-abstinent Trigaius a female companion, but Trigaius worries that it could be problematic if the woman becomes pregnant. Hermes assures Trigaius that his companion won't get pregnant if they use pennyroyal. Ancient Greek audiences would have immediately understood the reference, which was surrounded by suggestive double entendres and hilarious gestures, although modern audiences probably wouldn't get it without a footnote.

Pennyroyal also became a slang expression for pubic hair, as evidenced by yet another reference from Aristophanes, this one in *Lysistrata*. The play includes several references to well-groomed pennyroyal that has been plucked or singed to make the area more appealing.

Ancient Greeks didn't understand conception the way we do today. Many of them believed that only the man contributed genetic material, and that the woman was merely the incubator that brought the fetus to fruition. The line between contraceptive and abortifacient was blurred because of debate over when conception was believed to have occurred. (Sound familiar?) Pennyroyal was classified as an emmenagogue, but how was it used by the ancient Greeks?

There are several reasons a woman might want an emmenagogue. Her period might be irregular due to illness, famine, or stress, and regulation would make it easier for her to conceive. But if a woman were pregnant and did not want to be, an emmenagogue might bring on her period, terminating the pregnancy.

Pennyroyal is also believed to be the species of mint used in the kykeon, the potion drunk at the Eleusinian mysteries (*see* "Barley"). But why would the kykeon include a plant-based contraceptive, when Demeter (the Mysteries were an essential part of her cult) was so strongly associated with fertility? If pennyroyal was considered an emmenagogue, something that improves fertility by regulating menstruation, that makes sense. Or, if the mysteries included ritual sex (as some scholars suggest), then pennyroyal might have prevented a resulting pregnancy.

In addition to being a well-known contraceptive/abortifacient, pennyroyal was also an effective way to bring on or speed up childbirth, according to Pliny the Elder. Unfortunately, miscalculating the dosage could be a fatal mistake. Ancient texts refer to using pennyroyal in suppository or tea form, but modern chemistry allows the essential oils of pennyroyal to be distilled. This oil can be used safely as an insect repellent; however, it is much stronger than the water-based medicine used as a tea or suppository. Pennyroyal poisoning is still occasionally a problem among women who have swallowed the distilled oil.

Pulegone is the compound in pennyroyal that makes it effective as an emmenagogue and abortifacient. It is also found in catmint, peppermint, and spearmint, so obviously small amounts are safe to consume without ill effect. However, the FDA has banned synthetic pulegone as a food additive and classified the substance as a carcinogen. It can be toxic to the liver and lungs in large doses.

Recent research shows many of the herbs referenced as contraceptives in ancient literature are quite effective, but unregulated doses are risky. Because the amount of pulegone varies widely from plant to plant, it's difficult to calculate a safe dose outside of a lab. So while you should feel free to use pennyroyal oil to keep the mosquitoes at bay, it's a good idea to restrict yourself to external use.

A CULINARY ODYSSEY

Cornelian Cherry

Silphion

Lotus

Asphodel

Fig

Acorn

Cornelian Cherry

Cornus mas

The cornelian cherry appears in multiple Greek myths, valued both as food and for its wood. Also known as the cornel, its wood was famous for being hard, flexible, and durable. In *Enquiry into Plants*, Theophrastus describes its use in making javelins, while Herodotus tells us the Lycians (from modern-day Turkey) used it for their bows. Pausanias says the Greeks used cornelian cherry wood to build the Trojan horse. And Polydorus, the youngest son of King Priam of Troy, was killed by a spear of cornelian cherry wood.

In book 3 of the *Aeneid*, Virgil describes how Aeneas fled Troy and landed in Thrace, intending to start a colony there. He found a mound "overgrown with cornel" and began to harvest the plant to build a sacrificial altar. When he cut the first stem, he noticed blood dripping from the wound. Aeneas ignored the blood and continued to work, until he heard a groan and the sound of a man sobbing. It was Polydorus, who was sent to Thrace to live under the protection of the king while the war was fought in Troy. When it became clear that the Greeks would win the war, the Thracian king killed Polydorus and stole his treasure.

The ghost of Polydorus told Aeneas, "An iron hedge of spears covered my body, pinned down here, and the pointed shafts took root." And here's what makes this story special: Those spears really could have taken root! The cornelian cherry (*Cornus mas*) is actually a dogwood, not a cherry. (The common name comes from its large red fruit.) Dogwood cuttings root quickly and easily in moist soil, as anyone who has ever decorated a holiday container with cut dogwood branches knows. Within a few weeks those branches have rooted, confirming that the spears that killed Polydorus could, in fact, have rooted in place, pinning him to the spot for eternity.

The cornelian cherry tree is also part of the story of the infamous Gordian knot. Today, the Gordian knot is an expression used to describe a difficult problem, often solved with an unexpected, bold stroke. Originally it referred to an actual knot. The Phrygians (located in what is today western Turkey) were without a king, and an oracle predicted that the first man to enter the city in a wagon should be crowned. Some sources say that a farmer named Gordias was made king, and others claim it was his son Midas (yes, *that* Midas). Either Gordias or Midas dedicated the wagon to Zeus and tied it to a post near a temple with a strip of cornel bark.

Many years later another oracle said that anyone who could unravel the intricate knot would rule all of Asia. Alexander the Great did the deed, either by untying it, or just slicing it in half with his sword. And in fact, Alexander did conquer most of Asia, as it was known by the Greeks at that time.

As a food, cornelian cherries were both appreciated and disrespected, depending on the storyteller. In the *Odyssey*, Homer describes cornels as pig fodder. Circe fed the fruit to Odysseus's men, whom she had transformed into pigs with her sorcery.

But the human inhabitants of ancient Greece most definitely ate cornelian cherries. Excavations in the 1990s of a late Neolithic site (5400–4500 BCE) near the village of Makriyalos in northern Greece uncovered the remains of cornelian cherries along with acorns, figs, grapes, elderberries, and a variety of grains.

In Ovid's *Metamorphoses*, we find the story of Baucis and Philemon, ordinary mortals who welcomed Zeus and Hermes into their humble home when no one else would offer the disguised gods hospitality (*see* "Linden"). Baucis and Philemon were poor and had very little to offer their guests, but Philemon "set out . . . autumn ripened cornel cherry pickles."

In Eastern Europe and the Middle East, the cornelian cherry has been valued as food for thousands of years. Check the shelves of any Eastern European grocery store and you'll find cornelian cherry juice, cornelian cherries preserved in syrup, and whole, dried cornelian cherries. In Iran, cornelian cherries are used to make sharbat, a sweet-tart drink made by combining the fruit syrup with water.

In the United States, gardeners know the cornelian cherry as an ornamental flowering tree. It is one of the earliest trees to bloom in spring, producing delicate yellow flowers before the tree leafs out. The fruit ripens in fall, but most Americans leave it for the squirrels, and that is a shame. Cornelian cherries are ripe when they fall off the tree and are either deep red or yellow-orange, depending on the variety. They're exceptionally tart, with great flavor and loads of pectin, which makes them a jelly-maker's dream. Pig fodder indeed.

Silphion

In ancient Greece, the silphion plant had value comparable to silver and gold. It was expensive, limited in supply, and unique. Unfortunately, its value and desirability led to its extinction. Or did it?

The Greeks discovered this plant when they colonized the city of Cyrene in Libya, in the seventh century BCE. It very quickly became the most important trade item of Cyrene, so important that images of the plant were used on the city's currency. Silphion was food for humans and animals, and a medical panacea. A coin from Cyrene shows a woman touching a silphion plant and pointing to her genital area, indicating its usefulness in women's reproductive health.

The Greeks believed silphion could not be cultivated. It grew only in Cyrene and only in the wild. Theophrastus explains how silphion was harvested in order to preserve the rare and precious plant: "They fix carefully the proper amount to be cut, having regard to previous cuttings and the supply of the plant."

Alas, after the area became a Roman province in 96 BCE, the silphion situation slid downhill, fast. Previously, tenant farmers had harvested the plant carefully and protected it from grazing animals by erecting stone walls around silphion fields. Now, absentee landowners decided that raising livestock on the land would be more profitable. More importantly, the Roman governors of Cyrene were appointed for one-year terms, and their salaries were based on how much income they could generate from their provinces. They exploited silphion, harvesting without regard to the future. By the first century CE, Pliny the Elder reports that the very last stalk of silphion was given to Emperor Nero.

How do you identify a plant that no longer exists? We have the botanical description from Theophrastus, who lived during prime silphion time, and the coins from ancient Cyrene. Theophrastus describes the plant as "having a thick root, a stalk like fennel, and a leaf like celery." Most botanists agree that this puts silphion squarely in the middle of the genus *Ferula* (*see* "Fennel"), and until very recently, the best candidate for silphion was generally considered to be *F. tingitana*—or giant Tangier fennel. However, *F. tingitana* has a high ammonia content and its resin has a noxious smell, making it a poor choice for food.

Additionally, the flower stems of *F. tingitana* are arranged alternately on the plant's main stem, while the images we have of silphion—on coins and numerous clay statues unearthed during excavations of Cyrene—show the flower stems in opposite positions. The ancient images of silphion are highly stylized and shouldn't be considered as accurate botanical illustrations, but flower and foliage arrangement are important identification characteristics, and silphion was a well-known plant at the time. Ancient botanists would certainly have noticed this inaccuracy.

Enter Mahmut Miski, a professor of pharmacognosy—the study of drugs found in natural sources like plants, animals, and microbes—at the University of Istanbul, and the plant known as *F. drudeana*. This plant was first identified in 1909, although the link to silphion was not made until almost a century later, by Professor Miski. He has discovered more than thirty secondary metabolites in the plant's tissues, some of which have been proven to possess anti-inflammatory, cancer-fighting, and contraceptive properties.

Professor Miski has also studied the habitat where *F. drudeana* grows today. Remember, the Greeks claimed silphion would *only* grow in a very specific part of Libya. The two sites in modern-day Turkey where populations of silphion have been discovered are geographically unusual and have much in common with the ancient growing region for silphion. The modern Turkish sites receive regular snow melt and cool winter temperatures. The ancient Libyan silphion sites today are heavily forested, with fertile soil and rainfall of over thirty inches per year, unlike most of desertlike Libya. Why is this important? Professor Miski discovered that the seeds of *F. drudeana* require cold stratification to germinate. He was able to create these cold, wet conditions in his lab, but the combination of cool and wet was not easy to come by in the Mediterranean. The microclimates of the silphion locations, in both ancient and modern times, provide the right growing conditions for seed germination.

Difficulty of cultivation is just one of many elements that contributed to the extinction of silphion. Remember, overharvesting and grazing were recognized as problems in ancient times. Modern research has shown that *F. drudeana* is slow growing; it can take eight to ten years to flower. Additionally, once it flowers and produces seed, the plant dies.

F. drudeana ticks a lot of silphion boxes. It's difficult to cultivate, it shares the same requirements for growing conditions, it physically resembles ancient depictions of silphion, it's loaded with medicinal phytochemicals, and cooking experiments with *F. drudeana* have proven it is a delicious plant, unlike the ammonia-flavored *F. tingitana*. But until remnants of an ancient silphion plant can be compared to modern plant species, we can't know if silphion has been rediscovered. Fortunately, this isn't as impossible as it sounds. Maritime archaeology has uncovered many fascinating items, sealed in amphorae, deep in the holds of ancient shipwrecks, and the town of Cyrene had a port city, Apollonia, only eleven miles away. Perhaps a container of silphion resin lies at the bottom of the harbor, waiting to be discovered.

Lotus

Ziziphus lotus

On his way home from the Trojan War, Odysseus encountered sirens, monsters, and lovely young maidens, all of whom delayed his return to Ithaka. Once, after being blown off course, his ship stopped on the shores of what is modern-day Libya to replenish its water supply. Homer tells us they were in "the land of the Lotus-eaters, people who eat the lotus, mellow fruit and flower."

Odysseus sent a few men off to do reconnaissance, but they did not return. He sent a few more. They did not return either. Had they been attacked? Captured? Killed? No! They had been fed lotus fruit by the lotus-eaters.

> *Any crewmen who ate the lotus, the honey-sweet fruit,*
> *lost all desire to send a message back, much less return,*
> *their only wish to linger there with the lotus-eaters,*
> *grazing on lotus, all memory of the journey home*
> *dissolved forever.*

Odysseus's men had been drugged with a delicious, magical fruit, and now they wanted nothing more than to lie around on the beach, eating that fruit with their newfound friends. The lotus was an addictive, narcotic food that left Odysseus's men both stupefied and insatiable.

Without his men, Odysseus knew he wouldn't make it home. So he forced them back to their ships, their faces streaming with tears. He lashed them to their benches, and the few men who had not eaten the lotus fruit rowed the ships away from shore.

Imagine a fruit so delicious and so magical that all you want to do is loll around on the beaches of Africa, eating and soaking up the sun with your companions. What could that fruit be?

Writers have speculated on the identity of the mythical lotus for millennia. It was certainly not the plant we call lotus today. *Nymphaea caerulea* is a water lily; each flower produces a single, ovoid fruit, approximately two inches tall. It is native to parts of Africa, and its fruit may have a soporific effect in small doses, or a hallucinogenic effect in larger doses.

Herodotus reports that the lotus-eaters subsisted entirely on lotus fruit, even using it to make a sweet, strong wine. He describes the fruit as being smaller than a quarter inch in diameter and borne in clusters, with a flavor similar to that of dates.

Theophrastus gives a full description of the magic lotus in *Enquiry into Plants*. He describes the tree as the size of a pear tree with bean-size fruit that grows in clusters like grapes, changing color as it ripens. This description matches up well with that of the wild jujube, which grows in Africa. The wild jujube (*Ziziphus lotus*) is native to the Mediterranean. It grows best in hot, dry climates; sandy, fast-draining soils; and full sun. The fruit of the wild jujube changes from green to yellow to reddish brown and averages just over a half-inch long when fully ripe.

Diospyros lotus (the date plum) is a sweet and delicious fruit but is approximately three quarters of an inch in diameter. Is that too large to be considered bean-size, as Theophrastus described the lotus fruit? The answer is no. In Greece today "giant beans" measuring an inch long are a favorite dish. The date plum is not native to Greece or Africa, but it is grown in both places and is considered one of the oldest cultivated plants on record.

If we take the soporific effect of the blue lotus, combine it with the deliciousness of the date plum and with the tree height and fruit size of the jujube, then sprinkle it with some mythological enchantment, we'd have the magic lotus. If we're looking for an actual, real-life plant, the wild jujube is our best bet.

Its close relative, the cultivated jujube (*Z. jujuba*) is widely distributed around the globe and tolerates temperatures as low as –20°F (–28°C). It's considered easy to grow and is rarely bothered by pests or diseases. Like the wild jujube, it grows best in full sun with moderate moisture, in well-drained soil.

In the United States, the cultivated jujube is valued both as an attractive landscape plant and as a food crop, primarily in the Southwest. The fruit color changes from dark green to reddish-brown as it ripens, which matches up with the description of ripening fruit in Theophrastus. Eaten fresh, the jujube has a crisp texture; dried jujubes make a tasty snack and can be used in the same ways raisins and dates are used. However, it's a safe bet neither fresh nor dried fruit will make you forget where you live.

Asphodel

Asphodeline lutea, Asphodelus albus

Ask a gardener today if they grow asphodel and you'll probably get a blank stare in return. Yet the two plants we call asphodel today are both excellent perennial plants for a well-drained, full-sun garden and are hardy in USDA Zones 6–9. They are drought-tolerant bulbs, and like most bulbs, grow best in winter-dry regions, like those with a Mediterranean climate. Plants can grow to be three to four feet tall when in bloom, and the flowers of both species are fragrant. It's astonishing that such low-maintenance, gorgeous plants aren't seen more often in American gardens.

In ancient Greece asphodel was valued more for its edibility than its beauty. The plant was created by Demeter to feed Herakles as he traveled through the deserts of Libya en route to labor number eleven. The Pythagoreans (followers of the Greek philosopher and mathematician Pythagoras) considered asphodel to be a perfect food because it required no input from man, and they were right about that. Asphodel is a tough plant, growing in poor soils with very little water. Hesiod praised asphodel as a food in *Works and Days*, calling it a great blessing.

Theophrastus also extols the edible virtues of the plant:

It provides many things useful for food: The stalk is edible when fried, the seed when roasted, and above all the root when cut up with figs; in fact as Hesiod says, the plant is extremely profitable.

Yet despite its pretty flowers and its usefulness as food, asphodel is often associated with death in Greek mythology. In fact, an entire section of the underworld was named after this plant.

During the Classical Period (479–323 BCE), the Greeks' view of the underworld included three different sections. The truly evil were condemned to Tartarus for eternal punishment, while heroes and the relatives of immortals (like Helen of Troy, daughter of Zeus) lived happily in the Elysian Fields, aka the Islands of the Blessed. Everyone in between (which was most people) went to the Meadows of Asphodel, where they experienced neither joy nor pain.

In Homer's *Odyssey*, Odysseus travels to Hades to speak with Teiresias (the blind seer). After Teiresias advises Odysseus on how to reach his home on Ithaka, Odysseus stays to speak with the ghosts of family and friends. He finds heroes like Achilles and Orion in the asphodel meadows, but it is a dreary place where the soulless shadows of men wander, unsettled, with no memories of their earthly lives until they drink the blood of the sheep Odysseus has slaughtered. Odysseus finally leaves Hades, driven above ground by the ancient Greek version of a zombie apocalypse.

The dead came surging round me,
hordes of them, thousands raising unearthly cries,
and blanching terror gripped me—panicked now
that Queen Persephone might send up from Death
some monstrous head, some Gorgon's staring face!

No one is actually tortured in the asphodel meadows, but no one is happy to be there.

Some scholars suggest that ghostly pale, ash-colored asphodel flowers gave the grim meadows their name, but these scholars were clearly not botanists. Asphodel flowers are not ash-colored (gray); they are either sunny yellow (*A. lutea*), or bright white flushed with pink or violet (*A. albus*). A few ancient texts describe the foliage as gray, but this is also incorrect. Some species have green foliage, while others have blue-green leaves.

One clue as to why those scholars may have thought asphodel flowers were the color of ash can be found in the original Greek. In "Homer's Asphodel Meadow," Steve Reece points out the similarity in ancient Greek between "the asphodel meadows" and "the ash-filled meadows." The difference between asphodel and ash-filled in English is obvious, but the difference in ancient Greek is a single letter.

Additionally, the ancient Greeks generally burned their dead, turning them to ashes and releasing their souls. So the underworld might indeed be full of ashes, but not ash-colored flowers. And finally, flowers

are pretty and make people happy. Ashes are not pretty and do not make most people happy. Neither do the dead. You do the math.

Asphodel was often planted around graves, and the plant was sacred to both Hades and his wife Persephone. Hades (the god, not the place) was sometimes depicted holding fronds of asphodel, and Persephone was crowned with asphodel leaves in her cult on Rhodes.

Pliny the Elder, in his *Natural History*, lists fifty-one remedies involving asphodel, ranging from drying up putrid sores to soothing inflammations of the testes to making hair curl. He calls it "one of the most celebrated of all the plants" and even mentions that it makes a wholesome bread.

The foliage of both asphodels is still used in Greek and Turkish cuisine. It requires boiling to alleviate the bitterness, but many beloved greens (e.g., chicory, radicchio, and endive) are similarly bitter when eaten raw, so don't let this deter you. After cooking, the flavor of asphodel foliage resembles that of spinach. The roots are considered famine food by some, and a nutty-flavored potato replacement by others. The flower spike, prepared like asparagus, and the open flowers, added raw to salads, are quite tasty.

Asphodel honey is a specialty of modern Sardinia, a luxury item made exclusively from the flowers of wild asphodel. Its makers (the human makers, not the bee makers) tout the medicinal value of the honey, and there are numerous ongoing studies looking at the medicinal value of the plant itself, but asphodel is not currently being used in Western medicine. Pliny would be so disappointed.

Fig

Ficus carica

Kalchas was a famous Greek priest and seer. It was prophesied that he would die when he met a seer more gifted than himself, and for many years it seemed that would never happen. But then he met Mopsus, who challenged Kalchas to a duel of divination. They found a fig tree with a huge number of figs on it and Mopsus bet that he could predict the exact number of figs on the tree and exactly what the volume of the harvest would be. Mopsus was right, and Kalchas dropped dead on the spot, either from shock or shame.

The fig *(Ficus carica)* was so important in ancient Greece that there were special laws about who could harvest them and when. Sure, figs are delicious, but even more importantly, they are easily preserved by drying. This made them more valuable than most fruits, because like grapes (which could be either dried into raisins or made into wine), figs could be preserved for times when food might be scarce. In the *Laws*, Plato describes several rules governing the fig harvest:

» Anyone who picks figs before they are ripe must pay 50 drachmas to Dionysus if he picks from his own land, and 100 drachmas if he picks from his neighbor's.

» If an enslaved person picks figs without permission from the landowner, he will be whipped once for every fig he harvested.

» A foreigner (with a single attendant) may eat the fruit as he travels, as "a gift of national hospitality." (The Greeks thought hospitality to foreigners was so important that they had a word for it: *philoxenia*.)

Plutarch tells us that Solon, the sixth-century BCE Athenian lawgiver, entirely prohibited the export of figs from Attica (the region of Greece that includes Athens), and most classicists agree that the word *sycophant* derives from *syka* (figs) and *phainein* (inform), meaning those who informed on the illicit export of figs. Clearly the Greeks took their figs *very* seriously.

Figs were part of the big three in ancient Greece, coming after olives and grapes in importance as an agricultural crop. Archaeological evidence indicates figs were cultivated in Greece as far back as the early Bronze Age (approximately 3000 BCE). Figs grow quickly and can produce fruit within three to four years of being planted. But growing figs in ancient Greece was tricky. The tree doesn't form a traditional flower—the flowers are actually held *inside* the fruit. While some modern cultivars can produce fruit without pollination, in ancient Greece farmers had to devise a system to work around the complicated pollination process. Their system was called caprification and it's still practiced today by growers of certain fig species.

Here's how caprification works. Branches are cut from caprifigs, which are fig trees that produce unpalatable fruit containing male flowers. These small fruits ripen in spring and nourish the fig wasp; humans do not consider them edible. Farmers cut branches with these ripe but inedible figs on them and hang them on the branches of the trees forming true (tasty) figs, which ripen in fall. The emerging wasps from the caprifigs pollinate the female flowers of true figs. Kudos to the farmer who *fig*ured that out!

By the time of Theophrastus (the fourth to third century BCE), caprification was common knowledge, and he clearly describes the process in *Enquiry into Plants*: "Gall insects come out of the wild figs which are hanging there, eat the tops of the cultivated figs, and so make them swell." Theophrastus also comments on how easy it is to propagate figs from cuttings, which is current horticultural practice.

But figs were valued for more than their delicious fruit. Dioscorides tells us they are good for the bowels, dissolving tumors, and to treat tinnitus. Fig sap was (and still is) used as a rennet for making cheese. Socrates extols the virtues of fig wood for carving in Plato's *Hippias Major*. He mentions a pedestrian use of fig wood (making a ladle), but a more interesting use of fig wood relates to the god Dionysus.

In case you're wondering why Dionysus makes so many appearances in these pages, it's important to know that he was a vegetation god and had relationships with many different plants (*see* "Fennel" and "Ivy"). He was also a sexual god, in ways that were nontraditional in ancient Greece. At Dionysian celebrations, traditional gender roles were often inverted, and the sexuality of Dionysus himself was fluid. Which brings us to the story of Dionysus, Prosymnos, and the Phallus Made of Fig Wood.

This story is not commonly found in Greek mythology. The most complete surviving version of the story was told by Clement of Alexandria, a Christian theologian in the second to third century CE, in an effort to discredit pagan worship. In this account, when Dionysus wanted to rescue his mother Semele (*see* "Grape") from Hades, he asked Prosymnos for directions. Prosymnos agreed to help if Dionysus would have sex with him, and Dionysus said, sure, he'd come back as soon as he had retrieved his mother. When Dionysus returned,

Prosymnos had died, but Dionysus felt obliged to fulfill his part of the bargain. He carved a phallus out of fig wood and used it as a dildo on himself at the grave of Prosymnos.

Why fig wood? The fig was sacred to Dionysus, and figs were a common tree in ancient Greece with flexible, easy to carve wood. Wooden phalluses were essential elements in Dionysian rituals and are depicted in numerous pieces of ancient Greek pottery. Herodotus refers to their use in Dionysian festivals, and also describes the use of string puppets with outsize, moving sex parts at Dionysian ceremonies in Egypt.

And yet the fig was also a symbol of female sexuality. The fruit represented fertility because of its many seeds, and the shape and color of the fruit made it a convenient stand-in for the vulva. In Aristophanes's *Peace*, it is used for both sexes in the same line: "The bridegroom's fig is great and thick; the bride's very soft and tender." Clearly the fig is a very sexy fruit, and anyone who has enjoyed the seductive flavor and texture of a ripe fig might well agree.

Acorn

Quercus spp.

These days if you tell people you eat acorns, they look at you funny. They may even warn you that acorns are toxic. (Foragers are used to being teased for eating like squirrels by those who have never enjoyed the rich, delicious flavor of acorn flour.) But acorns have been a staple food around the world for millennia, and they were especially important before the cultivation of grains. In Thessaly, archaeologists have discovered the remains of acorns linked to human settlements that date from 6400–5600 BCE. The earliest testimonies of Greek acorn consumption date from the works of Hesiod and Homer in the Archaic Period.

In *Works and Days* (a treatise on farming and morality), Hesiod extols the virtues of the pastoral life and describes the generosity of the oak tree.

> *Famine and blight do not beset the just,*
> *Who till their well-worked fields and feast. The earth*
> *Supports them lavishly; and on the hills*
> *The oak bears acorns for them at the top*
> *And honeybees below.*

Homer, composing at about the same time, was nowhere near as impressed with acorns; he considered them food for pigs, not for men. In book 10 of the *Odyssey*, the sorceress Circe turns Odysseus's men into pigs: "Off they went to their pens, sobbing, squealing as Circe flung them acorns, cornel nuts, and mast, common fodder for hogs that root and roll in mud." Perhaps as someone who knew more about warfare than agriculture, Homer was unaware of just how tasty acorns could be.

Hundreds of years later, Socrates could have informed him. In Plato's *Republic*, Socrates describes acorns as a delicacy to be savored in an ideal society: "We'll set desserts before them—figs, pulse, and beans; and they'll roast myrtle-berries and acorns before the fire, and drink in measure along with it."

Socrates notwithstanding, most Greeks thought of acorns as food for animals and primitive peoples. The Arcadians were one of the original tribes to inhabit Greece (i.e., they were considered primitive), and in the third century BCE Apollonius of Rhodes describes them: "Arcadians who lived even before the moon, it is said, eating acorns on the hills." In *Fasti*, Ovid confirms that primitive humans ate acorns, but explains that grain, the gift of Ceres (the Latin name for Demeter), is a better food.

> *Later the acorn was known: its discovery was fine,*
> *Since the sturdy oak offered a rich horde.*
> *Ceres was first to summon men to a better diet,*
> *Replacing their acorns with more nourishing food.*

Ovid may have been a first-class poet, but he was no nutritionist. Acorns are highly nutritious and provide a significant source of fat, which is unusual for a plant. An article posted by the National Institutes of Health in 2020 shows acorns are "rich in unsaturated fatty acids and fiber, vitamin E, chlorophylls, carotenoids, phenolic compounds, and antioxidant properties."

Calories were hard to come by in the days of hunter-gatherers, and acorns were loaded with them. One hundred grams of acorn flour

provides 501 calories and 30.2 grams of fat, while 100 grams of whole wheat flour provides only 370 calories and 2.73 grams of fat. Acorn flour is also gluten free. Considering the number of people today who prefer gluten-free flours, as well as the popularity of the keto (high fat) diet, acorns may be on the brink of a comeback.

In ancient Greece, acorns were more than an important edible. Their caps were also useful (although not edible), and the biggest, most useful caps came from the Valonia oak. *Valonia* may be a corruption of the Greek word for acorn, βαλανός (pronounced vah-lah-nos), or may be derived from the Albanian port of Valona, which was originally a Greek colony and is now known as the town of Vlorë. The port was surrounded by Valonia oaks, and for centuries it exported Valonia acorn caps to tanneries throughout Europe.

"Why acorn caps?" you ask. The acorns of the Valonia oak (*Quercus ithaburensis* subsp. *macrolepis*) are huge (up to two inches in diameter) and quite unusual looking. Their caps are frilly and cover almost the entire large nut, and they contain large amounts of tannins. Tannins are what give acorns their bitter flavor, and they must be leached from the nuts to make most acorns palatable and safe to eat. Those same tannins are a useful, naturally occurring chemical, historically used in dyeing, making ink, and tanning leather.

Mostly replaced by man-made chemicals by the 1960s, tanning with Valonia acorn caps is making a comeback among artisanal tanners. Leather tanned with the acorn caps is considered more durable and resilient than chemically tanned leather and is also more colorfast and eco-friendly.

Acorns not only had practical uses in ancient Greece, but they were also symbols of sex and fertility, because the Greeks thought the acorn resembled the head of the penis. In Aristophanes's *Lysistrata*, the acorn is part of an elaborate sexual metaphor involving fitting a shaft into a hole. Jugs made in the shape of acorns were used for storing oil, and golden acorns were a decorative motif in libation bowls, jewelry, and magnificent Macedonian crowns made in the shape of oak leaves and acorns.

Today acorns are considered a nuisance by many gardeners. They sprout in the lawn, they're uncomfortable underfoot, and they bring deer into the garden. But ask any forager and they'll tell you that acorns are a plentiful and easy crop to gather, and once dried, the nuts last for years if stored correctly. After shelling, grinding, and leaching, acorns make a rich, gluten-free flour that can be used in any number of sweet or savory dishes.

Processing acorns is labor-intensive, although the invention of industrial nutcrackers and powerful blenders makes the work go faster than it did four thousand years ago. But the flour is tasty and nutritious, and the appeal of free food is undeniable. Perhaps it's time to revisit the pastoral diet of the Arcadians while we till our fields and worship the Olympians.

SHAPE SHIFTERS

Laurel

Plant
Metamorphoses

Mulberry

Pine

Linden

Moly

Laurel

Laurus nobilis

Zeus wasn't the only god with a wandering eye. His son Apollo gave him a run for his money, and it all began with a chance encounter in the forest, at least in Ovid's *Metamorphoses*. Apollo is strolling through the woods, having just slayed the Python, a giant snake/dragon, when he meets Eros (aka Cupid, god of erotic love and desire), the young son of Aphrodite. Eros is stringing his bow, and Apollo insults him.

> *What are* you *doing with such manly arms,*
> *lascivious boy? That bow befits our brawn,*
> *wherewith we deal out wounds to savage beasts . . .*
> *Content yourself with kindling love affairs*
> *With your wee torch—and don't claim our glory!*

Eros replied disrespectfully to Apollo (aka Phoebus),

> *Your arrow, Phoebus, may strike everything;*
> *mine will strike you: as animals to gods,*
> *your glory is so much less than mine!*

Then along came the nymph Daphne, in the wrong place at the wrong time. Daphne was a follower of Artemis and an accomplished hunter, sworn to remain a virgin. Eros drew two arrows from his quiver. He shot Apollo with a gold-tipped arrow that caused him to fall in love. He shot Daphne with a lead-tipped arrow that caused her to feel only fear and disgust. She fled, and Apollo, unused to rejection, tried to persuade her that he was worthy of her love, by bragging about his patrimony. (Jove is the Roman name for Zeus.)

> *You've no idea, rash girl, you've no idea*
> *whom you are fleeing, that is why you flee!*
> *I'm worshipped in the city of Patara!*
> *...*
> *Jove is my father.*

It is futile to flee from a god. When Daphne realized she would soon be caught, she cried out to her father, the river god Peneios, begging him to save her. Immediately she felt a numbness starting at her feet and rising upward as she transformed from nymph to laurel tree (aka bay laurel), her body enclosed in bark, her arms turned to branches, and her feet rooted in the ground.

Apollo embraced the tree and vowed to keep it sacred forever. He made the tree evergreen, giving Daphne a form of immortality, and ever after wore a crown of bay leaves in his hair. His lyre was carved from laurel wood, as was his quiver.

Another version of the story describes Daphne as the daughter of Amyclas, a Spartan king. One day, while she was out hunting, a youth named Leukippos saw her and fell in love. He disguised himself as a woman in order to enjoy Daphne's company, and they became fast friends. But Apollo also loved Daphne and was jealous of Leukippos. He inspired Daphne to bathe in a nearby spring with her attendants, but Leukippos would not join them. The women stripped him naked in what probably began in a high-spirited, teasing, slumber-party pillow fight kind of way, but when they saw he was a man, they killed him. Cue Apollo, who swooped in for his chance with Daphne. She fled, and just as she was about to be overtaken by the god, she begged Zeus to save her and he turned her into the laurel tree.

In other versions, it is Gaia who turns Daphne into the laurel and in some stories her father is Ladon, not Peneios the river god or Amyclas the Spartan king. But all versions end the same way, with the rescue of Daphne always being via metamorphosis into the laurel.

Many scholars insist, however, that the laurel tree was associated with Apollo long before he fell for Daphne. In his play *Hecuba*, Euripides shows us the captured Trojan women as they await their fates at the hands of the victorious Greeks. They speculate on what awaits them, wondering if they might end up as priestesses on Delos, the island where Leto gave birth to Apollo and his twin sister, Artemis. Would they serve on "Delos, sent by sea-oar to suffer life in the temple where palm and laurel sprang up at Leto's twinned birth pangs?" This puts the origin of the laurel at Apollo's birth.

One of the earliest Apollo myths involves the killing of the Python, a giant snake/dragon that terrorized the population surrounding what is now Delphi. Apollo slew the Python, then built the sanctuary at Delphi on top of the Python's body. But the Python was a child of Hera's, and she was not pleased that one of her husband's illegitimate children had killed it. To atone for this crime, Apollo had to be purified with laurel branches.

This is just one of many times laurel shows up in stories associated with Apollo, Delphi, and the Python. The priestess at Delphi was known as the Pythia, and earlier classical scholars speculated that she chewed laurel leaves to reach her prophetic state, although modern research shows that laurel leaves have no mind-altering properties. Apollo named the Pythian Games after the Python, and winners at the Pythian Games were crowned with laurel branches and leaves. (Women were allowed to compete in the Pythian Games, and an inscription records the victory of Tryphosa in the girls' foot race. If only Daphne had run as quickly as Tryphosa, she might have outrun Apollo.)

Laurel was a traditional purification herb in ancient Greece and was believed to protect against evil spirits. Just as Apollo purified himself with laurel branches, so was laurel used to purify Orestes, who killed his mother Klytemnestra (who killed her husband Agamemnon, who killed their daughter Iphigenia). In Euripides's *Ion*, Ion says as he purifies Apollo's temple, "Come fresh-blooming branch of lovely laurel, with which I sweep clean the precinct below the shrine." And in *Characters*, Theophrastus describes the superstitious man who chews on a laurel leaf for protection against unseen powers.

Dioscorides recommends laurel as an anti-inflammatory, an abortifacient, and to treat tuberculosis. While modern research has shown laurel to have anti-inflammatory and wound-healing properties, most of us use bay leaves as a cooking herb rather than as medicine.

Laurel is hardy to USDA Zones 8–10. It's an attractive evergreen plant, with dark green, leathery leaves. Laurel grows best in part shade with average moisture. Its foliage can be used fresh, or dried and stored for later use. Laurel can also be grown in containers as a houseplant, for gardeners who live where winters are too cold for it to survive outdoors. In containers the plant will rarely exceed 3–5 feet in height, but in its native habitat laurel can grow to be 10–30 feet tall.

In his *Description of Greece*, Pausanias says the oldest sanctuary of Apollo at Delphi was built with laurel boughs from the Vale of Tempe, a gorge said to be carved through the rocks of Thessaly either by Poseidon's trident or by Herakles, when he diverted the Peneios river to clean the Augean stables for his fifth labor. Does the name Peneios sound familiar? He was the father of Daphne, and we are back where we began.

Plant Metamorphoses

Being turned into a plant was surprisingly common in Greek mythology. Sometimes it was a reward for virtue, sometimes it was a punishment for hubris, and sometimes the resulting plant was a memorial to a lost loved one.

—— Crocus ——

Crocus sativus

There are two origin stories for the crocus. In one, Krokos was a mortal beloved by Hermes. They were throwing the discus one day when Hermes accidentally hit Krokos and killed him. Hermes turned Krokos into a flower and Krokos's blood became the bright stigmas of the saffron crocus.

Alternatively, Krokos was in love with the nymph Smilax. In some versions his love was unrequited and he killed himself. The first crocus sprouted from his grave. In others, because he was a mortal and Smilax was a nymph, they could not be together. The gods took pity on them and turned Krokos into a crocus, and Smilax into the smilax vine (*Smilax* spp.).

Today smilax is considered a thorny, annoying weed. It's best known for snagging on clothing as you walk through the woods. Foragers, however, know that the young tips of the smilax vine make a tasty trail nibble. In contrast, the saffron crocus is a much beloved, fall-blooming bulb that grows best in full sun. Each flower produces only three tasty stigmas, which must be harvested by hand, then dried. No wonder saffron is such an expensive spice!

—— Cypress ——

Cupressus sempervirens

Kyparissus was a beautiful young boy and beloved of Apollo. Ovid tells the story of Kyparissus's love for a stag with golden antlers and pearl earrings. Some say the deer was a gift from Apollo to his lover. Others say the deer roamed freely on the island of Kos, where Kyparissus lived. Either way, the youth and the deer were friends.

Kyparissus would show the animal the best places to graze, and the deer would let Kyparissus ride on his back. One day, during javelin practice, Kyparissus killed the deer accidentally. He hadn't seen where the stag was resting, hidden in the shady woods. Apollo tried to console his lover, but Kyparissus would not stop weeping; he asked the gods that he be allowed to mourn forever. Kyparissus was turned into the cypress tree and his tears were transformed into the beads of resin that the tree exudes.

The cypress tree has been associated with sadness and mourning ever since. In the *Aeneid*, Virgil describes how Aeneas decorates the grave of Polydorus with cypress boughs. Ancient commentaries on the *Aeneid* explain two reasons for this: 1) once a cypress tree is cut down, it will not re-grow from the roots. In other words, when it's dead, it stays dead. And 2) the strong fragrance of cypress boughs could effectively counter the stench of death when used on or near the funeral pyre. Pliny the Elder tells us the cypress is sacred to Hades and was often placed at the entrance of a house as a sign of mourning.

—— Heliotrope ——

Heliotropium spp.

The nymph Klytie loved the sun god, Helios. He loved her, too . . . for a while. But when he left her for the princess Leukothoe, a mere mortal, Klytie did not take it well. Some say she mourned the loss of her love passively, wasting away as she stared, unblinking, at Helios as he traveled the heavens.

Ovid tells us Klytie actively sought revenge and told Leukothoe's father of his daughter's indiscretion. Furious with her immodest behavior, the king ordered his daughter to be buried alive, and she died. But Klytie's grief was not assuaged. She sat outside naked, without eating or drinking, gazing at Helios. Eventually she put down roots and was transformed into a small, purple flower: the heliotrope.

In today's garden, the heliotrope is usually grown as an annual, although it's perennial in USDA Zones 9 and warmer. Its fragrant flowers do indeed rotate on their stems, following Helios as he crosses the sky.

—— Hyacinth ——

Hyacinthus orientalis

Hyakinthos was a beautiful Spartan youth, beloved by both Apollo and Zephyrus, the west wind. Hyakinthos preferred Apollo and one day, as they were throwing the discus (note to self: avoid discus-playing with gods), the jealous Zephyrus blew the discus off course, and it killed Hyakinthos.

Apollo was bereft and asked to be made mortal so he could join his love, but this was impossible for an Olympian. So he created the hyacinth flower from Hyakinthos's blood.

Thereafter, the Spartans held a festival honoring Hyakinthos that both mourned his death and celebrated his rebirth. Being killed by a discus may not have been a reward, but having a festival created to celebrate your life is some compensation.

—— Larkspur ——

Consolida ajacis

After Achilles was killed in the Trojan War, his mother, the nymph Thetis, proclaimed that Achilles's armor should go to the bravest of the Greeks. Odysseus and Ajax (the second-best Greek warrior after Achilles) both claimed the prize, having been the only two Greeks to defend Achilles's corpse.

Agamemnon awarded the armor to Odysseus and Ajax was furious. He wanted revenge. But Athena, Odysseus's protector, caused Ajax to go mad, and he hallucinated, believing that herds of livestock were the comrades who had betrayed him. He slaughtered them without mercy, and when he came to his senses, he was mortified and killed himself by falling on his sword. The larkspur sprang from his blood.

Many storytellers say that the flower bears the inscription "ai ai," which can either be considered the ancient Greek equivalent of "woe is me" or a form of the name Ajax. If you can find anything resembling those letters on the petals of a larkspur flower you deserve a gold star.

In ancient Greece, larkspur was considered a kind of delphinium. Even today taxonomists sometimes lump the two species together. Dioscorides describes both, recommending the delphinium to help heal scorpion bites, and the larkspur for kidney stones, jaundice, and GI upset. The modern medical establishment disagrees on the safety of either plant for internal use, but gardeners everywhere agree that the flowers are gorgeous.

—— Mint ——

Mintha spp.

Minthe was a nymph and Hades's concubine. When Persephone arrived in the underworld as Hades's queen, Minthe bragged that she was more beautiful than Persephone and that she would soon take Persephone's place as queen.

In some versions of the story, Persephone turned the nymph into the mint plant. In others, Persephone tore Minthe limb from limb. In yet another, Demeter trampled Minthe to death to preserve her daughter Persephone's rightful place as queen. Hades is credited for making the mint plant smell good, in fond remembrance of his concubine.

Pliny the Elder recommends mint as a remedy for a long list of ailments including cholera, gout, and worms breeding in the ears. He also believed it would prevent lascivious dreams, although Dioscorides says exactly the opposite, telling us it encourages lust! He also says it's good for the stomach and soothes vomiting and bile.

Modern research focused on the medicinal properties of mint shows that several species contain high amounts of antioxidants, which are being investigated for their ability to rid the body of free radicals. The antibacterial, antifungal, and antiviral properties of several mints are also promising medicinally.

Gardeners know that mint can be a bully and generally should be restricted to containers. Even then, mint may literally send roots out through the bottom of the pot in search of more soil to colonize. It grows best in full sun with regular soil moisture. As a culinary herb, mint can be used fresh or dry, and a mug of mint tea makes a gentle remedy for an upset stomach. Just like Dioscorides said it would.

—— **Reed** ——

Arundo donax

Pan, god of shepherds and hunters, was the son of Hermes, and appeared as half man, half goat. Pan fell in love with the nymph Syrinx, but she was a follower of Artemis, and determined to remain a virgin. As Pan chased Syrinx, she called out to the nearby river nymphs for help. They transformed her into river reeds just as Pan threw his arms around her, and as he sighed in disappointment his breath blew across the tops of the hollow stems and made a musical sound. Pan harvested the reeds, bound them together, and created the panpipe, also known as the *syrinx.*

The stems of *Arundo donax* are still used today both for panpipes and as reeds for woodwind instruments. Despite all of our modern technological advances, no man-made material has been developed that equals its performance quality. While amateurs may use plastic reeds, professionals reject those as inferior.

Transforming reed stems into instrument reeds is a long process, requiring months from harvest to drying to cutting to soaking to shaving. No wonder they're so expensive. But the unique cellular structure of the reeds allows them to diffuse vibrations with great efficiency; in other words, they really do make beautiful music. Current studies of the reed's chemical, biological, and physical properties are ongoing at the University of Reading in England, in hopes of developing an engineered alternative.

Metamorphosis was common in Greek mythology. Sometimes it was bestowed in answer to a prayer, sometimes it was a memorial, and sometimes it was forced upon the recipient, perhaps as a punishment. You never knew whom you'd meet in the woods or how a game of discus-throwing would turn out.

Mulberry

Morus spp.

I n book 4 of *Metamorphoses*, Ovid tells the story of Pyramus and Thisbe. They grew up next door to each other in Babylonia, but their parents were enemies and forbade them to meet. Being neighbors (and being children) they could not help but wonder about each other. Pyramus listened for Thisbe's laughter whenever she played outside, and Thisbe watched for Pyramus whenever he left his house.

As the years passed, their curiosity about each other deepened, and Pyramus and Thisbe discovered a crack in the wall that separated their homes. They began to meet, whispering to each other through the gap. Although they could not touch, they stood pressed against the wall where "their warm breath touched from lip to lip." When have headstrong, hot-blooded teenagers ever been able to resist forbidden love? They whispered passionate pledges and arranged to meet at the foot of a white mulberry tree outside the city.

Thisbe disguised herself with a veil and escaped her house unnoticed. She arrived first at the mulberry tree and as she waited, a lion came to the nearby spring. The lion was fresh from a kill, covered with blood. Thisbe fled, dropping her veil on the ground in her haste. The lion picked up the veil in its bloody jaws, then dropped it to drink from the spring and moved on.

When Pyramus arrived, he found the bloody veil and the lion's footprints and jumped to the worst possible conclusion. He blamed himself for Thisbe's death, grabbed his sword, and plunged it into his heart. "His spurting blood shot upward in the air" onto the white mulberry fruit, darkening its color. More blood flowed into the earth and was taken up by the roots of the tree, turning the berries purple.

Soon, Thisbe circled back to the tree, hoping to find that the lion had left and that Pyramus had arrived. Confused, she wondered if she was in the right place. Could this be the same tree? The mulberries had changed color, from white to purple. When she saw her beloved Pyramus wounded, she cradled him in her arms, calling his name. His eyes opened long enough to behold Thisbe before he died.

Thisbe found her bloodied veil and Pyramus's sword. She realized he had killed himself out of love and guilt, and declared they would never be parted again. She grabbed the weapon, plunged it into her own heart, and with her dying breath called out to their feuding parents and to the gods to let her lie with Pyramus for eternity.

The gods answered her prayers and changed the color of all mulberry fruit from white to purple as a tribute to Pyramus and Thisbe. Their parents buried the lovers' ashes together in a single urn.

It's a messy, bloody story and mulberries are a messy fruit. In fact, finding them splattered on the ground beneath the tree is an excellent way to know they're ready to harvest. A fully ripe mulberry will fall off the branch at the slightest touch and its flavor is deeply sweet, entirely without acidity. The flavor of a mulberry pulled from the tree will disappoint. The fastest way to gather ripe, delicious mulberries is to spread a sheet or tarp under a tree and shake the branches, letting ripe fruit collect below.

If you're in the market for a mulberry tree for your garden, read the plant tag carefully. Because some people consider the fruit to be a nuisance, new, fruitless cultivars of white mulberry have been developed. These are attractive shade trees, but they will disappoint those who hope for fruit.

Modern botanists, foragers, and gardeners agree that the fruit color of the white mulberry tree is changeable. In fact, this mutability may have been one of the inspirations for the myth. White mulberry trees do not always produce white fruit. The berries often (but not always) ripen from white to red to purple, changing color just as the fruit did in Babylonia, but without the bloodshed.

Pine

Pinus spp.

The pine tree has an exceptionally gory origin story. Not surprisingly, there are several versions, all involving castration and death. In *Fasti*, Ovid tells us that Attis caught the eye of the goddess Kybele, who asked Attis to serve as a priest at her temple. She required him to remain chaste and Attis promised he would. Alas, he fell in love with a nymph and broke his promise. A jealous Kybele killed the nymph and drove Attis mad; in his insanity, he castrated and killed himself. Kybele felt remorse and asked Zeus to bring Attis back to life, but instead, Zeus turned Attis into a pine tree. Kybele was ever after served by self-castrating, eunuch priests.

Too bloody? How about this one: Pan, the god of hunters and shepherds, was well-known for his indiscriminate libido. He chased the nymph Pitys, who had sworn to remain a virgin all her life, and as she fled from Pan, Gaia (Mother Earth), turned her into a pine tree to save her. The pine tree became sacred to Pan. An alternate version says Pitys was beloved of both Pan and Boreas (the north wind), and that Pitys chose Pan as her lover. In anger, Boreas threw Pitys off a cliff and killed her, and Gaia turned her into a pine tree. Perhaps not as gory as Attis's story, but not exactly a happy ending.

The hero Theseus also contributed to the violent history of the pine. En route to Athens to claim his birthright from the father he never met (*see* "Aconite"), Theseus met the bandit Sinis, who was also known as the Pine Bender. Sinis would accost passersby, then tie them to two bent-down pine trees and let the trees go, tearing his victims apart. Fortunately, Sinis was hoist with his own petard when Theseus tied Sinis to two pine trees and killed him, just as the bandit had done to so many innocent victims. Then Theseus slept with Sinis's daughter. You know, because he could.

Despite its associations with death and violence, some ancient Greeks appreciated the pine tree's virtues. Pan was often described as wearing a crown of pine boughs, so he could keep the memory of Pitys close at hand. The pine was also sacred to Poseidon (god of the sea) for several reasons. Its wood was resistant to decay and considered the best for shipbuilding. And its resin was used for sealing the cracks between ships' boards. Crowns of pine were awarded to winners at the Isthmian Games, which were dedicated to Poseidon.

The ancient Greeks considered pine trees to be fertility symbols because they were so plentiful. Pine boughs were essential offerings at the Thesmophoria, the ancient Greek fertility festival for married women that honored Demeter and Persephone. Several months before the Thesmophoria, pine boughs, cakes in the shape of male genitals (yes, really), and young pigs were thrown into chasms at Eleusis (*see* "Barley"). These were retrieved months later in a state of decay and combined with seed. It was believed this would bring a good crop. Sound crazy? When the seed was sown, the pines contributed organic matter to the soil, and may also have acted as a mulch.

Perhaps the best-known use of the pine was as the top of Dionysus's staff, the *thyrsus* (*see* "Fennel"). For years, scholars have discussed the composition and significance of the thyrsus. Did it represent the phallus, an important symbol of fertility among Dionysus's worshippers? Was it topped with a pinecone or crowned with a psychoactive mushroom? Did the plants composing the thyrsus have symbolic meanings? Most classicists agree that if the thyrsus was topped with anything, it was probably a pinecone, creating a connection between the god of wine and the pine tree.

The most obvious relationship between pine and wine is not the rhyme . . . it's the amphora. The amphora was a two-handled jar used to store oil, grain, and other foodstuffs, most often wine. Resin from different pines and firs was used to seal amphorae. It was also used to coat the inside of amphorae, which helped prevent the wine from oxidizing through the porous sides of the clay vessels. Theophrastus describes the different pines and firs that produce resin, how the resin should be gathered, and which resin was best for both flavor and consistency, suggesting the resin was useful not only for sealing the amphorae, but also for imparting flavor.

Anyone who has ever tasted retsina, the resinated wine for which Greece is famous, has tasted a bit of ancient history. Modern analysis of pottery that once held wine shows the presence of acids contained in Aleppo pine (*P. halepensis*), telling us that retsina dates back to the early Minoan period (approximately 2200 BCE). The terpenoids in resin protected the wine from being converted to vinegar. The retsina of years past could be harsh and reminiscent of turpentine, but today you can buy retsina with just a suggestion of resin flavor. It's the perfect chilled beverage for a hot, Mediterranean afternoon.

Pine resin wasn't the only valuable foodstuff ancient Greeks harvested from the pine tree. Excavations at Krania, in southern Macedonia, uncovered a tavern containing pine nut residue. The tavern dates from the Hellenistic period (323–31 BCE), and archaeobotanists have identified the pine nuts as the seeds of *P. pinea* (aka the stone pine), which still thrives in Greece today.

In Messene (southwestern Peloponnese), archaeologists have discovered the remains of burnt stone pine seeds dating from the third century BCE. These are believed to have been part of a sacrificial gift at the monument to a local hero. The nuts had not been cracked open or eaten, and pine nuts are aromatic when burned, making them an appropriate offering.

Pine nuts continue to be popular in modern Greek cuisine and are used in both sweet and savory dishes. You'll find them in dolmades, halva, and pine nut sauce, which is made by pulverizing pine nuts with garlic, olive oil, and a few herbs. It's served with meat and fish, and it is delicious!

Rumors of pine nuts' aphrodisiac qualities abound on the internet, but there is no reason to suspect any of them are true. However, a glass of chilled retsina served with dolmades stuffed with rice and pine nuts might be tasty enough to put you in the mood.

Linden

Tilia spp.

The linden tree has a complicated legacy. It was created as the result of an extramarital affair between immortals; it is a symbol of eternal, married love; and it's associated with Aphrodite and the gift of prophecy among Scythian soothsayers. Let's begin with the illicit affair between Kronos and Philyra.

Like his son Zeus, Kronos also had a penchant for the ladies. He lusted after his niece Philyra, daughter of the Titan Okeanos. Unfortunately, Kronos's wife Rhea caught them in flagrante delicto, and Kronos, in a panic, turned himself into a stallion and galloped off. Philyra went on to give birth to Cheiron the centaur, half man, half horse.

Most centaurs were lusty, drunken lawbreakers, shunned by polite society, but Cheiron was different. He was admired and respected as the teacher of Achilles and shared his knowledge of medicine, music, and hunting with several other ancient Greek heroes, including Jason, of golden-fleece fame, and Herakles, whose reputation for strength and fearlessness persists today. But as far as Cheiron's mother,

Philyra, was concerned, she had given birth to an abomination, and she prayed to be transformed to escape the shame of having birthed a monster. Either Kronos or Zeus obliged and turned her into the linden tree.

Philyra may have been the first metamorphosed linden tree, but she wasn't the last. Ovid tells the story of Baucis and Philemon in *Metamorphoses*, in which Baucis is transformed into a linden tree—but in a good and happy way, not out of shame. The story takes place in Phrygia, part of modern Turkey. It stands as an example of the ancient Greek concept of *philoxenia*, which translates as friendship to strangers. To refuse a stranger hospitality was not simply considered rude, it was an insult to the gods and went against the rules of civilized society.

One day, Zeus and Hermes were out having some quality father-son time, disguised as peasants. As evening approached, they began to look for a place to stay among the local villagers, but no one offered them hospitality until they reached the humble abode of Baucis and Philemon, a poor, elderly couple (*see* "Cornelian Cherry"). Baucis and Philemon welcomed the travelers. They offered the strangers food and wine, sharing what little they had. They entertained their guests with conversation, made them comfortable with cushions made of dried sedge, and washed their tired feet in warm water.

Eventually, Baucis saw that no matter how much wine she poured, her pitcher never emptied, and when she and her husband realized they must be in the company of two gods, they apologized for the paucity of their offerings. Zeus assured them they had nothing to apologize for and told them to climb the hill outside the village. When they arrived and looked behind them, they saw that Zeus had destroyed the village as punishment for the villagers' lack of hospitality. The only thing remaining was a temple where the home of Baucis and Philemon had once stood.

As a reward for their philoxenia, Zeus asked the couple what they wished for. They asked to be made guardians of the temple, and that they be allowed to die together when the time came. Zeus granted both wishes, and when the couple died, he turned Baucis into a linden tree

and Philemon into an oak. The trees stood by the temple, a monument to philoxenia and to enduring love.

In *The History*, Herodotus describes how the Enarei (elite Scythian priests) used linden bark. Traditional Scythian soothsayers used willow to make their prophecies, but the Enarei split flexible linden bark into three pieces, then braided and unbraided them to divine the future. They believed this technique to be a gift from Aphrodite.

Today the linden is appreciated as a lovely shade tree and an excellent source of pollen, especially for honeybees, which are drawn to the copious amounts of nectar produced by the flowers. Linden honey has a unique scent and flavor, making it a popular gourmet item. Linden species are quite cold-hardy (the American linden is hardy to USDA Zone 3) and grow best in full sun and rich, well-drained soil. The linden makes a lovely specimen tree but will form a grove if suckers are not removed regularly.

Lindens are not only beautiful to look at, they also have several edible parts. Tender young leaves don't have much flavor but are good for filling out a stir-fry or salad. The flowers are the real treasure. They are not merely edible but have a lovely vanilla flavor and a slight natural sweetness. They make a tasty syrup for cocktails or to use as a base for sorbet. Herbalists use the flowers to make a tea considered helpful with digestion, muscle aches, and headaches, but the infusion is most often used as a calming, nonaddictive sleep aid. So the next time you find yourself tossing and turning, brew yourself a calming cup of linden tea with a dollop of linden flower honey. Perhaps you'll dream about the gods.

Moly

Galanthus nivalis

Moly is the most magical, mysterious, and mythological plant in ancient Greek literature. To this day, scholars and botanists disagree on what moly may have been. Most believe the plant was fictional, but historically the leading, real-life candidates have included cyclamen, various alliums, squill, mandrake, snowdrop, and wild rue. Fortunately, we can eliminate several of these right off the bat by looking at a few ancient descriptions.

Moly makes its first appearance in the *Odyssey*, when the sorceress Circe turns Odysseus's men into pigs. Odysseus, unaware of their fate, goes in search of them. He is met by Hermes, who tells him how his men have been transformed, and warns Odysseus about Circe's power.

> *Here, take this antidote to keep you safe*
> *when you go to Circe's house. Now I*
> *will tell you all her lethal spells and tricks.*
> *She will make you a potion mixed with poison.*
> *Its magic will not work on you because*
> *you have the herb I gave you.*

. . . The bright mercurial god
pulled from the ground a plant and showed me how
its root is black, its flower white as milk.
The gods call this plant Moly. It is hard
for mortal men to dig it up, but gods
are able to do everything.

Homer tells us that the gods call it moly, implying that humans have no word for it, or that, if humans know the plant, they might call it by another name. Also, we are told that the plant is easy for gods to harvest, but not for mortals. In other words, this is a powerful, mysterious, divine plant.

Several hundred years later, in *Enquiry into Plants*, Theophrastus mentions moly, and adds descriptive information he obtained from root-gatherers, the men who made a living harvesting roots for medicine or magic.

They say that this plant is like the moly mentioned by Homer, that it has a round root like an onion and a leaf like squill, and that it is used against spells and magic arts, but that it is not, as Homer says, difficult to dig up.

We now have several physical characteristics to go on: a black root that is round like an onion, a white flower, and a leaf like squill. From this alone we can remove mandrake, wild rue, and cyclamen from the running, although cyclamen does have a bulbous tuber, a white flower, and has been used to clear poisons from the system. Pliny the Elder states cyclamen could counteract spells, giving it magical properties, but the foliage doesn't match up with Theophrastus's description.

Historically, many scholars have guessed moly is in the onion family, and *Allium moly* (*Allium* is the onion genus) was named after the mythological plant. Allium foliage and bulbs match up with moly's description, and there are some alliums with white flowers. However, alliums were well-known in ancient Greece, both as food and as medicine. There's no reason to give a well-known plant such a mysterious moniker. Additionally, no mention is made by either Homer or Theophrastus of the distinctive smell that every allium plant has. It's a key identification characteristic today and was certainly a key identification characteristic thousands of years ago. Anyone who has ever smelled garlic or onion knows how strong and obvious the scent is.

The sea squill (*Drimia maritima*) is native to Greece, has white flowers, a large bulb, and leaves like a squill (strap-like with parallel veins). It has been used medicinally and as rat poison for millennia. Theophrastus makes two mentions of squill's magical properties, saying that a squill planted by the door of a house "wards off mischief," and that a superstitious man might "summon priestesses whom he bids purify him with the carrying around him of a squill." So sea squill is a valid candidate: white flower, onion-like root, squill-like leaves, magical/medicinal powers.

But even *more* interesting is *Galanthus nivalis*, the common snowdrop. The name itself provides a clue: *gala* = milk, and *anthus* = flower, i.e., it has a flower "white as milk." Additionally, it is a spring ephemeral and dies back to the ground shortly after blooming. For eight to nine months of the year the snowdrop is not visible above ground. Perhaps this is why it was difficult for men to dig up, but not for gods.

The plant is native to Greece, it has a round bulb, and its leaves are similar to that of squill. The snowdrop contains galantamine, a chemical that can improve cognitive ability. It is currently being used in patients with mild to moderate Alzheimer's, and while it is not a cure, it can help with the ability to think. Galantamine can also be used to counteract certain intoxicants that cause hallucinations.

In the *Odyssey*, Hermes gave moly to Odysseus to protect him from Circe's magic, so he would not be turned into a pig, like his crew members. Modern medical scholars propose that Odysseus's men were not *really* turned into pigs, but that they had been poisoned with some kind of intoxicant that caused delusions, amnesia, and hallucinations. In other words, they could have *imagined* they were pigs. This is an example of a phenomenon called anticholinergic intoxication.

Recent research shows that galantamine could indeed be a treatment for anticholinergic intoxication. A number of plants native to the Mediterranean can cause this kind of intoxication, including mandrake (*see* "Mandrake") and henbane (*see* "Flying Herbs"). So Circe, being an expert herbalist, could have used one of those plants to intoxicate Odysseus's men, then brought them back to themselves by administering an antidote of moly.

Some scholars suggest that *moly* was a general term for a magical plant, and if moly is entirely mythic, we can leave it at that. But often myths are based on real knowledge, which is then embellished to make it more entertaining and memorable. Could an herbalist in ancient Greece have caused a group of men to have mass hallucinations? Yes. Could that same herbalist have administered an antidote? Also yes. Was that antidote moly? Maybe. Were Odysseus's men turned into actual pigs? Nope.

GIFTS FROM
THE GODS

Fennel

Olive

Three Trees

Oak

Ivy

Rose

Fennel

Foeniculum vulgare, Ferula communis

Two different fennel plants make appearances in Greek mythology: common fennel (*F. vulgare*) and giant fennel (*F. communis*). One was valued as food, and the other changed the course of humankind.

Giant fennel lives up to its name and can grow to be ten feet tall. Its history is as impressive as its height. Let's start with Prometheus, Zeus's cousin. Despite being immortal, Prometheus had a soft spot for humans. He thought it was unfair of Zeus to deny humans fire, forcing them to shiver as they ate their meat raw. So he took a stalk of giant fennel to Mount Olympus, snuck into Hephaestos's workshop (the god of fire and metallurgy), stole a burning ember, hid it inside the fennel stalk, and brought it back to earth as a gift to mankind. Theophrastus describes the thick pith of giant fennel in *Enquiry into Plants*. This pith truly does allow a burning ember placed inside of it to smolder; the plant does not catch fire.

Zeus was furious. He couldn't kill Prometheus, because Prometheus was immortal, but he could make Prometheus *wish* he were dead. Zeus had Prometheus chained (or nailed, depending on the storyteller) to a rock in the Caucasus mountains, where every day an eagle would tear out his liver and eat it. Every night, Prometheus's liver would grow back, preparing him for another day's torture. Good times.

Despite his centuries of torture, Prometheus knew he would someday be freed. The name Prometheus translates to "forethought." Prometheus could see the future and knew exactly what fate held in store for him before he brought fire down to earth. Yet he did it anyway. Perhaps because he also knew that ultimately he would make a bargain with Zeus, who grudgingly allowed his son Herakles to kill the eagle and free Prometheus.

Scholars offer varying interpretations of this myth. Was the fire literal, or did it stand for enlightenment, meaning that Prometheus's true gift to man was intelligence and creativity? In *Prometheus Bound*, Aeschylus tells the story of Prometheus's torture, which some contemporaries interpreted as a political statement, casting Prometheus as the rebel and Zeus as the tyrant. Sometimes it's safer to tell a story with a hidden message than it is to directly criticize a government.

Giant fennel also appears in association with Dionysus, god of wine. Dionysus carried a staff called a *thyrsus*, which was made from a stalk of giant fennel, twined with ivy and topped with a pinecone. Why was fennel chosen for the staff? Why not something sturdier, like a tree branch?

In his *Bibliotheka Historica*, Diodorus Siculus explains:

> *When wine was first discovered, the mixing of water with it had not as yet been devised and the wine was drunk unmixed; but when friends gathered together and enjoyed good cheer, the revelers, filling themselves to abundance with the unmixed wine, became like madmen and used their wooden staves to strike one another.*

Dionysus was upset by this, although he did not decide that humans should refrain from drinking unmixed wine, because the drink gave such pleasure. Instead, he ordered the drinkers to carry a stalk of giant fennel

rather than a wooden staff. A thyrsus made from a fennel stalk couldn't cause as much damage as a piece of wood.

Sometimes the thyrsus served as a tool. Dionysus's followers, the maenads (*see* "Grape") used the thyrsus as a magic wand to produce water, wine, or honey—when they weren't tearing mortal men limb from limb, that is.

Common fennel grew in abundance on the battlefield of Marathon, where the Greeks defeated the Persians in 490 BCE despite being vastly outnumbered. The nearby village was named for the plant, which was known as *marathos*. Ancient Greeks served fennel with their olives, thereby savoring the memory of one of their greatest military victories along with the fruit of their signature tree.

Dioscorides recommended common fennel for a wide range of ailments, from inflamed kidneys to snake bite. This actually may have worked. Research published in 2014 by the National Library of Medicine (part of the US National Institutes of Health) shows common fennel to have strong antiviral, antimicrobial, and anti-inflammatory properties. It continues to be investigated for the development of new drugs and clinical uses.

Common fennel has the same anise flavor we get from bulb fennel (*Foeniculum vulgare var. azoricum*) but doesn't form bulbs. Still, the flowers, seeds, foliage, and pollen are all useful in the kitchen. Flowers and seeds can be used fresh or dried. Pollen should be preserved by drying and can be stored in an airtight container for up to a year. Foliage is best used fresh.

Giant fennel is a common weed in Greece today, towering over the heads of passersby. It is not generally considered edible, primarily because there are two visually indistinguishable strains, one of which is considered medicinal and the other, which is considered toxic, capable of causing significant hemorrhaging. Is that a chance you're willing to take?

Olive

Olea europaea

The olive tree is quintessentially Greek. Its association with Athens dates back to the birth of the city itself. Before Athens was Athens, it was ruled by the mythical king Kekrops, who was a man from the waist up and a serpent from the waist down. Kekrops was said to have been born from the soil of Attica, making him an original, indigenous Greek. Many hallmarks of civilization were credited to Kekrops (laws of marriage, the first census, abolition of human sacrifice), but most important to plant lovers is the story of Kekrops and the olive tree.

In some versions of this story, King Kekrops wanted to appoint a patron god for his new city. In others, the gods themselves decided to claim various towns and cities as their own. In every version, the two contenders for possession of Athens were Poseidon and Athena. (There will be no surprise ending here. The city isn't called Poseidontown.) Both gods were asked to give a gift to the city; whoever gave the better gift would become the patron god.

Poseidon hit the ground with his trident, and a spring of salt water gushed forth. Athena either dug a hole in the ground and planted an olive seedling, or struck the earth with her spear, turning the weapon itself into an olive tree. One version tells us that the Olympians chose the winner. Another says the decision was left to the voting populace, and that the men voted for Poseidon while the women voted for Athena. Since there was one more woman than there were men, Athena won. That version of the story tells us it was after this loss that the men of Athens decided women should no longer be allowed to vote.

Athena clearly deserved to win. Sure, water is essential for life, but Poseidon was god of the ocean, i.e., salt water. What use was salt water? You couldn't drink it, you couldn't wash with it, you couldn't water fields and gardens with it. Olives, on the other hand, were incredibly useful. Their wood was valuable, their fruit was a popular food, and their oil was used for cooking, lighting, and grooming. Poseidon didn't have a chance.

Athena's olive grew on the grounds of what would become the Acropolis, and olive trees continued to be planted there for centuries. The trees on the Acropolis were owned by the state, and uprooting one was punishable by banishment or confiscation of property. In the sixth century BCE, the Greater Panatheniac Games were established, and unlike many other athletic contests, where the winners were crowned with garlands of leaves, winners of the Panatheniac Games were given a much more valuable prize. They won olive oil made from the sacred trees of the Acropolis, all of which were believed to be descended from the original olive tree that had been the gift of Athena.

Athena may have shared a bit of her immortality with her sacred olive tree. After the Persians captured Athens, in 480 BCE, they burned the temple on the Acropolis, including Athena's olive tree. Herodotus tells us that the next day, the tree had already put forth new growth, becoming a symbol of hope for all of Greece.

In ancient Greece, olive oil was used for more than cooking. It was burned as fuel in lamps and used in ointments by athletes before their competitions. Olive oil anointed the bodies of fallen heroes, and in the *Iliad*, when Hera wanted to seduce Zeus (to prevent him from seeing

what was happening on the battlefield of Troy), she massaged herself with olive oil, making herself irresistible to her husband.

> *Hera cleansed her enticing body*
> *of any blemish, then she applied a deep olive rub,*
> *the breath-taking, redolent oil she kept beside her . . .*
> *one stir of the scent in the bronze-floored halls of Zeus*
> *and a perfumed cloud would drift from heaven down to earth.*

The wood of olive trees also plays a prominent role in ancient Greek mythology. Herakles used an olive tree as his club, and Odysseus fashioned a spear made of olive wood to blind the cyclops Polyphemus, who held him and his men prisoner. The olive tree in its entirety plays an important role in the *Odyssey*. When Odysseus reveals himself to Penelope after a twenty-year absence, she doubts his identity. He proves himself by describing the bedroom and bed he built for her lo these many years.

> *Who could move my bed? Impossible task,*
> *even for some skilled craftsman—unless a god*
> *came down in person, quick to lend a hand.*
> . . .
> *There was a branching olive-tree inside our court,*
> *grown to its full prime, the bole like a column, thickset.*
> *Around it I built my bedroom.*
> . . .
> *Then I lopped the leafy crown of the olive,*
> *clean-cutting the stump bare from roots up,*
> *planing it round with a bronze smoothing-adze—*
> *I had the skill—I shaped it plumb to the line to make*
> *my bedpost. . . .*

Archaeological evidence from the southern Peloponnese and the island of Santorini shows that olive wood charcoal has been used by people inhabiting Greece for more than ten thousand years. By the time of Homer, the process of tending olive trees was well understood. In the *Iliad*, Homer uses a young olive tree in an analogy to describe a soldier, felled by Menelaus:

> *There he lay*
> *like an olive slip a farmer rears to strength*
> *on a lonely hilltop, drenching it down with water,*
> *a fine young stripling tree, and the wind stirs it softly,*
> *and it bursts with silver shoots—*

In *Oedipus at Colonus*, Sophocles describes the olive tree with admiration and reverence. Clearly it is more than a mere tree in the Mediterranean landscape.

This plant truly flourishes in our land,
the grey-leafed olive tree, nurturing
our country's youth. No young person here
will lift a hand to damage or destroy it,
nor any citizen living with old age,
for it's guarded by the ever-watchful gaze
of grey-eyed Athena and protector Zeus.

Today, vast orchards of gray-leafed olive trees stretch for miles in Greece. And while no one may be building their bed around an olive tree or seducing a god with olive oil–massaged skin, the olive and its oil remain essentially Greek. And essentially delicious.

Three Trees

In ancient Greece, trees could be many things. Some were oracles that spoke (*see* "Oak"). Some were sacred to a god (*see* "Laurel"). Some were used to win a war (*see* "Cornelian Cherry"). And some were used for food or medicine. Some were even homes to nymphs, whose lives were tied to the lives of their trees. The ancient Greeks venerated their trees for many reasons.

Ash

Fraxinus spp.

The meliai were ash-tree nymphs who sprang from the blood of Ouranos (the original god of the heavens) when he was castrated by his son Kronos. When the blood reached Gaia (Mother Earth), she gave birth to the meliai—who in turn gave birth to the men of the Bronze Age, a warlike race that was eventually destroyed in a giant flood. But before that, the meliai armed their sons with spears made of ash wood. Ash wood is lightweight compared to oak, but almost as strong and dense, making it an excellent choice for weaponry.

Cheiron the centaur gave Peleus a spear made from ash at his wedding to Thetis, and Peleus's son Achilles took this spear with him to the Trojan War. Homer describes the weight of the spear in the *Iliad*:

> *No other Achaean fighter could heft that shaft,*
> *only Achilles had the strength to wield it well:*
> *Pelian ash it was, a gift to his father Peleus*
> *presented by Chiron once, hewn on Pelion's crest*
> *to be the death of heroes.*

Several other warriors in the *Iliad* fight with ash spears, including Aeneas and Menelaus. Nemesis, the goddess of retribution, is sometimes depicted holding a branch of ash, although there are no accounts of her using it as a weapon. Perhaps her judgments were as sharp as a spear made from ash wood.

But the ash tree wasn't used exclusively as a weapon. The Greek word for the manna ash (*Fraxinus ornus*) is *melia*, which is not only similar to the name for the ash-tree nymphs—*meliai*—but also is very close to the Greek word for honey, *meli*. The manna ash was valued for the sweet liquid that oozed from cuts made in the bark of the tree. Pliny describes a delicious, sweet substance found on trees that most scholars interpret as manna. He calls it "the perspiration of the sky or a sort of saliva of the stars," and says the bees consume it and turn it into honey.

Today, mannitol is a sugar alcohol derived from commercially cultivated manna ash trees, primarily in Calabria and Sicily. Mannitol is naturally sweet but poorly absorbed by the human intestine, making it a low-calorie sweetener useful for diabetics. It is also used medicinally as a diuretic to treat glaucoma and elevated intracranial pressure. The ash can cure as well as kill.

—— Poplar ——

Populus spp.

This story is rated R . . . consider yourself warned. In his "Hymn to Demeter," Callimachus tells the story of Erysikhthon, a king of Thessaly who disrespected Demeter's sacred grove—with deadly consequences.

One day, Erysikhthon brought twenty giant men into Demeter's sacred grove to harvest wood for a banquet hall. They first attacked a poplar tree that was especially beloved by all the nymphs who lived in the grove. With the first strike of the axe, the tree's resident nymph cried out in pain, and Demeter rushed to earth in the form of her priestess. She spoke gently to Erysikhthon, warning him that he risked making Demeter angry, but Erysikhthon threatened her with his axe in return. At that, Demeter showed herself in her true form and the giant men fled. Demeter let them go (they were just following orders), but cursed their king to always be hungry, no matter how much he ate or drank in his banquet hall.

In *Metamorphoses*, Ovid takes the story further. He tells us that when King Erysikhthon had exhausted his wealth attempting to satiate his endless hunger, he sold his daughter, Mestra, so he might buy more food. Not surprisingly, Mestra did not appreciate being enslaved. She ran from the man who had bought her, begging Poseidon for help. He gave her the gift of shape-shifting and she took on the appearance of a fisherman, which so confused her new master that he left without her. When Erysikhthon realized Mestra could change her shape, he continued to sell her over and over, to feed his gluttony, and Mestra continued to escape in various forms, both human and animal, until the day she went off to the island of Kos with Poseidon and bore him a son.

Eventually even this was not enough, and Erysikhthon began to eat himself, consuming first one limb, then another, until he died. Demeter's vengeance was fierce indeed.

— Yew —

Taxus spp.

The Erinyes (aka the Furies) were a scary bunch. As goddesses of vengeance, they were particularly concerned with crimes against parents and against the gods, and their favorite punishment was to drive the guilty party mad. Like the meliai (ash-tree nymphs) they were born from the blood of the castrated Ouranos.

The Erinyes are often portrayed carrying torches of a "blazing yew branch," and there are numerous mythological links between the yew tree and death. The yew was sacred to Hekate (goddess of witchcraft and associated with the underworld) and was also linked to Artemis, who is said to have dipped her arrows in poison made from yew. In Plutarch's *Moralia*, the characters discuss the effects of wearing garlands at drinking parties. Trypho warns against the powers of garlands and reminds his fellow diners "that even the shade of a yew kills men who sleep in it." Fear not, it is most definitely safe to sleep in the shade of a yew if you are so inclined.

Theophrastus was aware that yew foliage was poisonous to humans and beasts, but he also knew that the fruit was sweet and safe to consume. He does not, however, mention that the seed inside the fruit must not be swallowed, for it is toxic, like the foliage.

Today, the anticancer drug Taxol is derived from the bark of several yew species (*Taxus* spp.). Taxol works by blocking cell division and is especially effective against breast and ovarian cancer. Yet another example of a plant that can either kill or cure.

Oak

Quercus spp.

When you hear the word *oracle*, you probably think of Delphi, where an intoxicated woman muttered poetic riddles that were interpreted by priests who may or may not have had ulterior motives for their translations. But the oracle at Dodona was much simpler than that. It was the oldest oracle in Greece. It wasn't a woman or a priest. It was an ancient, imposing oak tree, considered by some to be the personification of Zeus. In the earliest days of the cult, people believed that Zeus lived inside the tree.

Dodona is in northwestern Greece, in the region of Epirus. So far off the beaten track, the oracle at Dodona didn't have the kind of notoriety that Delphi did, nor did it elicit the same kind of inquiries. Statesmen and politicians went to Delphi with far-reaching questions about wars and plagues. But Dodona was a humble oracle, and the majority of its hopeful applicants were local inhabitants. Their questions related to everyday life. "Am I really the father of my daughter?" "Will I be successful raising sheep?" Archaeologists have discovered thousands of lead tablets inscribed with questions like these, to which the oracle would give a simple yes or no answer.

How the oak tree issued its prophecies changed over time. In the beginning, the tree is said to have spoken, directly answering those who posed questions to it. The tradition of the talking oak was established early in Greek mythology. The story of Jason and the Argonauts is said to take place circa 1300 BCE, a century before the Trojan War. Jason built a ship called the *Argo* in order to sail to Colchis and retrieve the Golden Fleece. Athena herself took a branch from the sacred oak at Dodona and added a timber made from the branch to the *Argo*. The timber spoke to the Argonauts, warning them of danger and instructing them on how to best proceed with their quest.

Homer referred to Dodona in both the *Iliad* and the *Odyssey*, but by then the way the oracle spoke had shifted. In the *Odyssey*, Odysseus describes how the oracle at Dodona delivers "the will of Zeus that rustles forth from the god's tall leafy oak." But not everyone could understand the rustle of the leaves and therefore, translation was required. The first translators were priests known as the Selloi, and in the *Iliad* Homer describes their unusual habits.

> *Zeus, lord of Dodona's holy shrine,*
> *dwelling far away, brooding over Dodona's bitter winters!*
> *Your prophets dwelling round you, Zeus, the Selli*
> *sleeping along the ground with unwashed feet . . .*

Dodona is remote, located in the north of Greece where winter is cold. Dodona is also mysterious. The Selloi slept on the ground and did not wash their feet, which set them apart as primitive and strange. But lest you disrespect the Selloi for their lack of personal hygiene, remember that asceticism has always been common among monastic orders, and sleeping on the ground is not much different from sleeping on a wooden board. The Selloi believed they drew their power from the earth and that this made their interpretation of Zeus's prophecy possible.

Fast-forward another few centuries, and Herodotus tells us that the oracle at Dodona had changed almost entirely. Answers were delivered by priestesses (known as doves) who had taken the place of the male Selloi, and who may or may not have been interpreting the cooing of *actual* doves that lived in the oak. The tree itself, while still venerated as sacred to Zeus, no longer spoke or rustled its leaves prophetically. Later still, answers to applicants' questions were provided by lots, drawn by the priestesses.

Excavations at Dodona show a large hole next to the temple of Zeus, where archaeologists believe the sacred oak stood. The tree was not merely cut down; its root system was dug up, obliterated. This probably happened circa 380 CE, when the Byzantine emperor Theodosius made Christianity the official religion of the empire and banned worship at pagan sites.

Oak trees were often inhabited by dryads, nymphs whose lives were tied to their host trees. Dryads were joyous creatures who loved their trees and rejoiced in their company. But another story in *Metamorphoses*

tells us of women with a very different relationship to oak trees. Dionysus's female followers, the maenads (*see* "Grape"), were furious with Orpheus, a Thracian poet and musician, because he worshipped Apollo over Dionysus. Also, after the death of his wife, Orpheus was so devastated that he rejected women altogether, preferring the company of men. The maenads took this personally and attacked Orpheus, tearing him limb from limb. But Orpheus had once been a priest of Dionysus, and the god was angered by the maenad's violence against his former follower. He changed each maenad into a tree, "her grieving hand would strike her thighs, she strikes an oak; of oak is her breast made, and oaken are the maenad's shoulders too."

The oak at Dodona was a Valonia oak (*Quercus ithaburensis* subsp. *macrolepis*; *see* "Acorn"). This is a long-lived species and often grows to an impressive size. The largest existing specimen today is estimated to be more than seven hundred years old. Its canopy covers more than eight hundred square yards, and the diameter of its trunk at chest height is more than four feet. The Valonia oak is native to the Balkans and parts of the Mediterranean, and botanists believe it was one of the first oaks to be domesticated. Today, on the Greek island of Kea, this same species is an important agricultural crop, providing several economically important harvests.

Oak trees sequester large amounts of carbon, their roots assist with groundwater filtration, and their dead leaves shelter beneficial insects and add nutrients to the soil. Today, we value oaks for their strong and beautiful wood, for the shade and architectural form they provide in the landscape, and for the shelter they offer to insects, animals, and birds. Although no one has yet reported finding prophetic doves among the branches.

Ivy

Hedera helix

The grape was the plant most sacred to Dionysus, god of wine, but from the day he was born, Dionysus also had a strong connection to the ivy plant. Immediately after emerging from Zeus's thigh, Dionysus was crowned with ivy, then given to the nymphs of Mount Nysa for protection. Hera wanted to destroy Zeus's illegitimate child, but the nymphs hid him from the angry goddess, covering Dionysus's cradle with ivy leaves as camouflage.

Ivy was associated with Dionysus in many other ways as well. Vases that portray him almost always include ivy leaves in their design. Dionysus and his followers carried staffs called *thyrsi* (singular *thyrsus*), composed of a stem of giant fennel (*see* "Fennel") entwined with ivy. Ivy is also often mentioned as a wine additive in ancient Greece, once again linking the plant to the god of wine.

As a young god Dionysus traveled widely. Once upon a time, he wanted to sail from the island of Ikaria to the island of Naxos. One version of the story says he hired a ship that turned out to be manned by pirates; another version says pirates kidnapped him from Ikaria. But in no version does anyone ask why a god needed a ship to get from point A to point B.

The pirates mistook the beautiful young Dionysus for a wealthy prince and decided to hold him for ransom. Two ancient authors (Hyginus, as well as Servius in his commentary on the *Aeneid*) indicate that the pirates not only wanted ransom but were so thrilled by Dionysus's beauty that they planned to have their way with him. When it became clear that the pirates had no intention of delivering Dionysus to Naxos, the god began to toy with his captors. Calmly, he slipped out of the ties that bound him (made from slim chaste tree branches), at which point the helmsman realized this must be a god. He pleaded with the captain to release Dionysus, but the captain was greedy and would not listen. Mysteriously, a grapevine grew from the topmost sail and, as described in the Homeric hymn to Dionysus: "Then round the mast dark ivy twined / luxuriant with flowers and lovely growing berries."

Ovid tells us that the ivy bound the oars and sails, and that Dionysus brandished a spear twined with vine leaves. Next, he turned himself into a lion, which prompted the captain and crew (except for the helmsman) to jump overboard. Dionysus turned them into dolphins, but spared the helmsman, who became one of Dionysus's followers.

Ivy was described as having magical properties in Nonnus's *Dionysiaca*, where it is used both as a weapon and as a life-saving medicine. In the poem, Dionysus is said to have conquered India (where they disrespected him by not worshipping him or drinking wine), and in the detailed and very gory accounts of battle, ivy is used to slash human flesh. The mere touch of ivy can split open a suit of armor.

Another shot at the foe with flesh-cutting ivy; no sword he had, no round buckler, no deadly spear of battle, but shaking clustered leaves of plants he killed the mailed man with a tiny twig.

Yet just a few pages later, when Dionysus's favorite young soldier is wounded, Dionysus "gave the boy new life with his healing ivy." So which is it? A terrifying weapon or a miracle cure? Probably neither.

Theophrastus describes several types of ivy, but makes a mistake in assuming that different physical characteristics indicate different plant species. Immature ivy has slim, flexible stems, lobed leaves, and a climbing or creeping growth habit. It does not flower or fruit. Mature ivy develops thick woody stems, the leaves are spade shaped, and it produces flowers that are followed by dark blue/black fruit. It may take up to ten years for a plant to reach blooming age, and frequent pruning can keep ivy in its juvenile state indefinitely. In other words, immature ivy looks and grows very differently from mature ivy, so let's cut Theophrastus some slack.

Several other classical writers offer descriptions of ivy. In *Moralia*, Plutarch's characters debate whether ivy is cold by nature, thus dampening the effect of wine, or whether it is hot in nature, thereby making wine more intoxicating. Pliny the Elder lists thirty-nine conditions that ivy was used to treat, ranging from diseases of the nostrils to tape worm to dysentery.

Hippocrates recommends boiling ivy root, then grinding it into a powder and combining it with flour and white wine to make a poultice for inflamed rectal prolapse. And while that may sound like an unusual treatment, contemporary herbalists do use ivy for its anti-inflammatory properties. A modern over-the-counter ivy leaf extract has been shown to improve symptoms of bronchial inflammation; it works by liquifying mucus, then acting as an expectorant. More studies are currently underway investigating other ways ivy leaf extract might be used to treat inflammation. It has thus far been shown to inhibit chronic arthritis in rats and chronic asthma in mice.

Today many gardeners avoid planting ivy outdoors, for several reasons:

» It's considered invasive in several states and classified as a noxious weed in the Pacific Northwest.

» Where ivy is evergreen, birds and mice make their nests behind the leaves.

» The flowers of mature plants attract an impressive quantity of bees. (Pro? Con? You be the judge.)

But when people blame ivy for destroying a building's exterior, they're going too far. Consider all those giant manor houses in Great Britain, covered with ivy, yet standing solid for centuries. Ivy anchors itself to trees and structures with rootlets that act as suction cups. If a structure's surface is sound, ivy's suction cups won't do damage. However, if there are already cracks in stucco, wood, or masonry, the suction cups may further the damage.

Indoors, ivy remains a popular houseplant with numerous cultivars bringing variegation and a range of leaf shapes to the windowsill. It's an easy plant to grow in bright, indirect light, and tolerates a drafty spot. Let the top half-inch of soil dry out between waterings.

And the next time you're having a cocktail party, fashion yourself a crown of ivy, then pour a libation to Dionysus. The gods appreciate a respectful gesture, so why not get at least one of them on your side?

Rose

Rosa spp.

For more than three thousand years, the rose (*Rosa* spp.) has been a symbol of romantic love. The flower is soft, fragrant, voluptuous, and sensual. In contrast, its stem is painfully prickly and can draw blood. So it makes sense that the rose was sacred to Aphrodite, goddess of love, well-versed in both pleasure and pain.

Equally familiar with both the beauty and pain associated with the rose is Eros, often considered to be Aphrodite's son. Some say Aphrodite was born pregnant with Eros, others say Eros was one of the oldest gods and preceded Aphrodite. Either way, the rose was often also associated with him. One story tells how Eros was stung by a bee hidden inside a rose, then ran to his mother complaining he had been killed, "struck by the small winged snake that farmers call the bee." Aphrodite reminded him that a bee sting was far less painful than the pain inflicted by his own arrows.

The best-known story about Aphrodite and the rose involves the death of Adonis (*see* "Lettuce"). And of course, there are several versions. Bion's "Lament for Adonis" says that the rose sprang from Adonis's blood and the anemone from Aphrodite's tears. In *Metamorphoses*, Ovid says that Aphrodite sprinkled Adonis's blood with sweet nectar, and that the combination formed the blood-red anemone flower—a flower with a very short lifespan, just like Adonis.

While Aphrodite certainly appreciated the rose for its physical charms, she also knew it had medicinal properties. Near the end of the Trojan War, Achilles, champion of the Greeks, killed Hector, prince of Troy. It was a yearslong rivalry and Hector had just killed Patroclus, Achilles's beloved friend. Achilles was wild with rage, and he took it out on Hector's corpse. He stripped the body of its armor and pierced Hector's heels with rawhide, then tied him to his chariot and dragged him around the walls of Troy, again and again, as Hector's family watched from the walls of the city. Achilles refused to bury Hector; he wanted the dogs to feed on the corpse, but Aphrodite had other plans. Hector had always been one of her favorites, so she anointed his body with "ambrosial oil of roses" to protect his skin so it would not tear as it was pulled through the dirt. Recent research shows that rose hip oil is significantly effective both as an anti-inflammatory and in wound healing.

The rose wasn't only useful on the battlefield. Some ancient Greeks believed that wearing a garland of roses at a drinking party would prevent drunkenness. The *Anacreontea* is a group of lyric poems written between the first century BCE and the fifth to sixth century CE. Most of the verses focus on love and romance and the rose makes a frequent appearance.

> *Let us mix the Loves' rose with Dionysus: let us fasten on our brows the rose with its lovely petals and drink, laughing gently.*

and

> *At feasts, banquets and festivals of Dionysus what should we do without the rose?*

The gardens of Midas were famous for their beautiful roses—before he turned them to gold. Herodotus tells us that roses grew wild in that region, "each with sixty petals and a fragrance superior to all other roses." Turning his fragrant roses into sterile golden flowers was only one of the things Midas regretted.

In *Natural History*, Pliny the Elder describes a dozen different varieties of rose, as well as how to best propagate, plant, and grow them. He cites thirty-two remedies derived from the rose, including treatments for diseases of the rectum and insomnia. He also suggests charring rose petals and using them as a cosmetic for eyebrows.

Dioscorides gives a recipe for making rose oil in *De Materia Medica* that calls for a thousand rose petals and multiple pressings with olive oil; you must coat your hands with honey before stirring the mixture up and down. He recommends taking the resulting oil internally for constipation and for breaking up mucus. Both Dioscorides and Pliny say that the rose is an effective cure for toothache pain, and modern medical studies of rose oil confirm it is an effective analgesic when applied topically.

Theophrastus goes into great detail describing the parts of the rose. He knew that cuttings produce plants faster than seed and understood how climate affects the beauty and scent of the flowers. In *Concerning Odors*, he describes the light but penetrating scent of rose oil, and its use in the most desirable perfumes. Some ancient Greek rose references were less refined. Comic playwrights of the fifth century BCE used the word *rose* as a stand-in for the female genitals, and *rosychest* referred to a girl's breasts.

Many people today don't realize that roses are edible, but during World War II, the British government paid children to collect rose hips, which were processed to make syrup, an important vitamin C supplement. Rose hips are still used to make *nyponsoppa*, a traditional Swedish soup. Rose petals are a common ingredient in Middle Eastern and Indian cuisines. Turkish delight is made from rose water, and the spice blend ras el hanout often includes dried, ground rose petals. If you decide to cook with rose petals, remember two things: 1) be sure not to harvest from anywhere that may have been sprayed with toxic chemicals, and 2) only fragrant rose petals have flavor.

As a garden plant, the rose may be the most beloved, most fretted over flowering shrub on the planet. And while the climate of Greece is perfect for roses, many gardeners elsewhere struggle to keep their roses healthy. High humidity brings on fungal diseases, and numerous insects love roses as much as gardeners do.

Plant breeders introduce multiple new rose cultivars every year. Unfortunately, their emphasis is often on disease resistance and reblooming. Of course, those are excellent qualities in a plant, but in the breeding process, fragrance is often sacrificed. And what is a rose without its heady, seductive scent? Aphrodite would not be pleased.

DIVINE TRICKERY

Apple

Narcissus

Pomegranate

Myrtle

Apple

Malus spp.

n Ovid's *Metamorphoses*, Aphrodite tells us of her sacred grove where the apples are made of gold; they are irresistible to humans and gods alike. These apples are instigators, setting in motion stories of love, infidelity, and war. These apples are *not* something you'd pack in a lunchbox.

Consider the princess Atalanta. Her father wanted a son to inherit his kingdom, not a daughter, so he ordered her to be abandoned in the wild, exposed to the elements. Rescued by a bear and raised by hunters, Atalanta became famous for slaying licentious centaurs, hunting mythical beasts, and making water spring from a stone by striking it with her spear.

Ovid writes that Atalanta received a prophecy telling her that marriage would be her doom, so she forswore men, dedicated herself to virgin Artemis, goddess of the hunt, and went to live alone in the woods. But when news of her fame reached her father, he claimed Atalanta as his daughter and insisted she marry.

Despite the whole "you must die because you are a girl" thing, Atalanta forgave her father and agreed to wed. However, she would only marry a man who could best her in a footrace, and anyone who failed to beat her must die. (In some stories Atalanta did the executing herself.) But because Atalanta was a generous soul, she gave every suitor a head start.

Several suitors died trying before Hippomenes showed up. He arrived as a curious spectator, but as soon as he saw Atalanta, he was smitten. He knew he couldn't outrun her, so he prayed to Aphrodite, goddess of love, for help. She gave him three golden apples from her sacred grove and told him how to win Atalanta in marriage.

The race began and Atalanta soon took the lead. Hippomenes pitched an apple into her path and Atalanta slowed to scoop it up, falling behind. She caught up with Hippomenes, who lobbed a second piece of fruit. Again, Atalanta fell behind, picked up the apple, and regained the lead. Finally, Hippomenes threw his third piece of golden fruit. Atalanta retrieved it and lost the race.

Was she just a silly girl who couldn't resist three golden trinkets? That doesn't jibe with Atalanta's independent character. Maybe there's another explanation.

In ancient Greece, the apple was sometimes considered an aphrodisiac with magic powers. In his comedy *Clouds*, Aristophanes uses the expression "struck with an apple" to describe someone overcome with lust. So, when Hippomenes threw Aphrodite's golden apples, he was actually casting a divine love spell on Atalanta. How could she resist?

The best-known story about golden apples involves the Trojan War. Eris, goddess of discord, tossed a golden apple with the inscription "to the fairest" into a gathering of the gods. This caused an uproar as Aphrodite, Hera, and Athena each claimed the prize for herself.

No god dared arbitrate, so Zeus appointed Paris, prince of Troy, to be the judge. Each of the three goddesses offered a bribe in exchange for the apple, with Aphrodite promising Paris the most beautiful woman on earth: Helen. Apparently no one stopped to consider that Helen was married to Menelaus of Sparta—perhaps not even Helen herself. She fled Sparta with Paris and sailed to Troy.

Did Helen and Paris have a choice? The answer is no. The *Cypria*, an epic poem written in the sixth century BCE, describes the abduction of Helen, setting the stage for the *Iliad*. Sadly, that poem no longer exists, but happily, the Greek writer Proclus summarized eleven books of the *Cypria* in the *Chrestomathy*. There we learn that Zeus planned the Trojan War in order to relieve the overpopulated earth of her burden. The apple was a divine tool, conceived to wreak havoc among humans. Just as Atalanta couldn't resist the seductive power of Aphrodite's golden apples, so were Helen and Paris powerless to change their fate once Zeus decided there must be war and used the golden apple to get the ball rolling.

As for edible apples (*Malus* spp.) in ancient Greece, they were probably nothing like the large, sweet fruit we enjoy today. While the Greeks traded for what they called sweet apples (similar to our cultivated apples), they didn't have the right climate to grow them. Modern cultivated apples require between five hundred and a thousand hours at temperatures below 45°F (7°C; called chill hours) to form flower buds. This would have been difficult to achieve in the warm climate of ancient Greece. It's also why most commercial apples in the United States today are grown in cool or cold climates.

Most likely the apples that grew in Greece were crabapples (also *Malus* spp.). Crabapples are very closely related to regular apples, but do not require the same high number of chill hours as sweet apples do. However, crabapples are much more tart than cultivated apples and are substantially smaller. By definition, crabapples must be less than two inches in diameter.

Most modern gardeners consider crabapples to be ornamental trees, valued for their flowers. But the fruit of larger crabapples can be as crisp and juicy as any store-bought fruit. Crabapples are super high in pectin, making them an excellent fruit for jelly. They also make a tart and tasty fruit leather, an excellent applesauce, a spicy fruit pickle, and they infuse beautifully in bourbon. As foragers know, crabapples can be delicious, although no one has yet started a war with one.

Narcissus

Narcissus spp.

When modern gardeners look at a narcissus they feel happy and optimistic. Spring is here! The sun is out! The weather is getting warm! For the ancient Greeks, however, the narcissus (aka the daffodil) wasn't such a cheery symbol. In Greek mythology the narcissus was often associated with stories of abduction, separation, terror, death, and suicide.

Persephone was the daughter of Demeter (goddess of the harvest) and Zeus (king of the gods). Demeter and Zeus were also brother and sister, but the gods had different rules about that kind of thing. One day, Persephone was out picking flowers with her posse of nymphs when she saw an amazing narcissus with one hundred flowers. As she reached for the blooms, the ground beneath her opened and Hades, god of the underworld, appeared in his chariot, grabbed Persephone, and brought her to his kingdom beneath the earth where he intended to make her his wife and queen of the dead.

The beguiling narcissus was no earthly plant. It had been created specifically to lure Persephone away from her friends by the same god who approved the kidnapping plot: Persephone's father, almighty Zeus.

Fortunately, in this instance Zeus turned out not to be quite so almighty after all. Persephone's mother, Demeter, had some fierce bargaining power on her side, and managed to get her daughter back aboveground for at least part of the year (*see* "Pomegranate").

Persephone wasn't the only maiden seduced by a narcissus. In the story of Europa, Zeus entraps the beautiful princess with the same plant. Like Persephone, Europa was picking narcissi with her friends. The fun didn't last for long. Following the trail of irresistible blooms (placed there by Zeus), Europa was separated from her friends, then seduced by the god in the form of a white bull. He fled with her across the water to Crete, where she bore him three sons including Minos, who became ruler of the island. In a fascinating example of karmic payback, Minos's wife fell in love with an actual bull and had sex with it, giving birth to the minotaur, a half man, half bull. Minos imprisoned the minotaur in a labyrinth until Theseus killed it with the help of Minos's daughter Ariadne. All because Europa followed a trail of narcissi.

But wait, there's more. The Erinyes (aka the Furies) were three fierce sister goddesses who sprang from the blood of Ouranos when he was castrated by his son Kronos. The Furies were charged with punishing humans who committed crimes against nature, like violation of the laws of hospitality; disrespecting elders; and matricide, patricide, and fratricide. They drove humans mad, they punished entire cities with famine and disease, and they tortured criminals consigned to Tartarus (the worst part of Hades). They wore snakes in their hair and blood dripped from their eyes, yet the narcissus was sacred to them. It seems a jarring combination, but the narcissus was often associated with death, since it was instrumental in bringing Persephone to the underworld.

The narcissus itself was named after an arrogant young man, son of the water nymph Liriope. In *Metamorphoses*, Ovid tells us that Liriope consulted the seer Tiresias about her son Narcissus. Tiresias said Narcissus would live a long life if he never knew himself. Typical soothsayer obfuscation.

There are several versions of the story of the young man Narcissus, and none of them end happily. In one, the nymph Echo fell in love with him and was rebuffed. Bereft, she wasted away to nothing, until only her voice remained. In another version of the story, the youth Ameinias fell in love with Narcissus, and Narcissus responded by sending him a sword with which Ameinias killed himself. As he died, Ameinias asked the gods to teach Narcissus a lesson. Nemesis, goddess of retribution, heard his request.

One day Narcissus passed a pool of water in the woods and stopped for a drink. In the still waters of the pool he saw the most beautiful young man, and immediately fell in love. Ovid says Narcissus didn't realize it was his own reflection, and unable to tear himself away from the object of his desire, he wasted away and died. In another version he knew he'd fallen in love with himself and understood he would never be able to consummate his passion, so he killed himself. In both stories, the narcissus flower sprang from his dead body.

Today, there are hundreds of species and cultivars of narcissus, ranging from petite multiflowered varieties to large-cupped, single-flowered plants. Some are demure, pale yellow and white; others are vibrant egg-yolk yellow, orange, or red. Narcissi are harbingers of spring, and especially useful to those who garden in deer country—the plants are rarely bothered by animals since both their flowers and bulbs are considered toxic.

Some people cut or tie back their narcissus's foliage when the plants finish blooming, and while this may make your garden look neater, it's not great for the plant. Those leaves need to photosynthesize to store energy for next year's blooms, and by removing the leaves, or reducing the surface area exposed to the sun, you are decreasing the amount of nutrition the plant can produce and store for next year.

Narcissi are long-lived, pest-resistant plants with glorious flowers that give great pleasure to gardeners around the globe. No kidnappings, no suicides, no eternal punishments. Just fragrance and beauty.

Pomegranate

Punica granatum

After Hades abducted Persephone (*see* "Narcissus"), her mother, Demeter, wandered the earth, heartbroken. She asked everyone she met if they had seen her daughter. Did anyone know where she went? The Olympian gods were afraid to betray their brothers Hades and Zeus, but Helios (the Titan sun god) had observed the kidnapping from his chariot in the sky. He was *not* afraid and revealed the truth to Demeter.

In her anger and sorrow, Demeter, goddess of the harvest, forced the earth to suffer with her by causing famine. She allowed no seeds to germinate, no crops to grow, no food to be harvested. Very quickly Zeus realized that if mankind starved there would be no one left to worship the immortals, and he begged Demeter to relent. She refused. And since no god can reverse another god's magic (it's in the rulebook), Zeus commanded Hades to return Persephone to her mother so that human life on earth could continue.

Hades had no choice. Or did he? He agreed to send her back, but first he devised a cunning plan in order to retain Persephone's company for at least part of every year. The Homeric hymn to Demeter tells how Hades fed Persephone "a honey-sweet pomegranate seed . . . so that she might not spend all her days again with dark-robed, revered Demeter." Then he sent Persephone back to earth. She had no idea that the seeds she had eaten were more significant than a tasty snack.

Persephone and Demeter rushed into each other's arms. Then Demeter looked her daughter in the eye and asked if she'd eaten anything while she was away. Demeter knew what her daughter did not: Those who eat in the underworld, stay in the underworld. Persephone confessed that Hades had fed her pomegranate seeds. She didn't realize that for every seed she ate, she would have to spend one month beneath the earth, as Hades's queen.

Scholars disagree about how many seeds Persephone ate, but the consensus is that Persephone eating these seeds is why we have winter. When Persephone is underground, Demeter mourns, and the earth is barren. When Persephone returns, the earth is fertile again. Simple enough, but as a symbol, the pomegranate is complicated, often representing contradictory ideas or being used to achieve opposing results. For example, ancient Greeks considered the pomegranate to be both a fruit of the dead (responsible for the barren season on earth) *and* a symbol of fecundity (for its womb-like shape and blood-red liquid). It was used in wedding ceremonies as a hopeful symbol of the bride's fertility, yet Soranus of Ephesus (a Greek physician of the second century CE) describes six ways to use the pomegranate as a contraceptive. Medicinally it was used both as a laxative and as a cure for diarrhea.

There are multiple stories about the origin of the pomegranate. Some say it sprang from the blood of Dionysus the first time he was killed, or maybe the blood of Adonis, who only died once (*see* "Lettuce"). Others claim it was planted by Aphrodite on the island of Cyprus. And while the pomegranate was indeed often associated with Aphrodite as a symbol of sexuality and fertility, it was also claimed by Hera, goddess of marriage, to whom fertility was essential. Athena and Artemis were sometimes depicted with pomegranate fruit, although for reasons unrelated to human sexuality. Artemis, as goddess of the hunt, was responsible for the fertility and propagation of animals. For the warrior Athena, the fruit is considered an attribute of mature womanhood. Hestia, goddess of the hearth and the least well-known of the original twelve Olympians, wore pomegranate earrings and gave out pomegranate fruit as blessings. All goddesses had some sort of relationship with the pomegranate because all goddesses were immortal and the pomegranate was a symbol of regeneration, i.e., a cycle of life that does not end. But primarily, the pomegranate belongs to Demeter and Persephone. At the Thesmophoria married women fasted, eating only pomegranate seeds as they reenacted scenes from the story of Persephone and Demeter. If a seed fell to the ground they could not eat it, because that meant it belonged to the dead.

Today the pomegranate is a high-end fruit, widely touted for its health benefits, although the US Circuit Court of Appeals for the District of Columbia has told the folks at POM Wonderful they can no longer claim their pomegranate juice will reduce risk of heart disease, prostate cancer, and erectile dysfunction. While the juice is available throughout the year, pomegranate fruit generally ripens in fall and winter in the northern hemisphere.

Dwarf pomegranates are popular houseplants and will flower well indoors if given enough sun. But unless you hand-pollinate their flowers, the plants won't produce fruit. And while technically edible, dwarf pomegranate fruit has none of the sweetness of its larger cousin.

In the garden, pomegranates are full-sun plants. Most are hardy only in the warmer parts of the United States (USDA Zones 7–10), where they are used as landscape plants, valued for their flowers and fruit. Several new cultivars developed in Russia are more tolerant of cold climates, although they may die back to the ground at low temperatures, resprouting in spring, just like Persephone.

Myrtle

Myrtis communis

Aphrodite is a demanding goddess; she requires gifts and adulation, and woe to those who disappoint her. In Euripides's *Hippolytus*, the goddess of love curses Hippolytus because he vows to remain a virgin. In doing so, he insults Aphrodite, who then causes Phaedra, Hippolytus's stepmother, to lust after her stepson. All does not end well. Phaedra hangs herself, Hippolytus is killed by Poseidon, and sadness reigns.

Pausanias says that in Troezen, where Euripides's play takes place, there is a racecourse close to a shrine to Aphrodite. He says that Phaedra used to hide at the shrine and watch Hippolytus exercise (presumably in the nude, since that's how the Greeks exercised), and that she used her hairpin to puncture the leaves of the myrtle that grew nearby. Was she taking out her anger at Aphrodite on one of the goddess's sacred plants, or was she venting her sexual frustration on the innocent myrtle leaves? Either way, myrtle foliage is indeed covered with numerous transparent dots. These are oil glands that produce the fragrance and flavor for which the plant is valued.

Ovid tells us that when Aphrodite rose naked from the sea, sprung from the severed genitals of Ouranos, she covered herself with myrtle branches to protect herself from the lecherous gaze of the satyrs. (Satyrs were woodland deities with the ears and tails of horses or goats, depending on the story. They were obsessed with sex and rarely asked for consent.) Ovid also says that Aphrodite touched his forehead with a myrtle branch to inspire him, and he encourages prostitutes to offer myrtle to Aphrodite to make them charming, beautiful, and witty.

In Aristophanes's *Lysistrata*, the women of Athens withhold sex from their husbands in order to end the war with Sparta. A provocative scene takes place between Myrrhine (whose name means "little myrtle") and her husband. As he begs her to have sex with him, she tortures him by pretending to acquiesce, only to string him along in a series of highly seductive maneuvers, then leave him in the lurch. Later in the same play, men from Sparta and Athens, who can barely walk because of their erections, complain that the women won't let them "touch their myrtle" until the war is ended.

In *The Deipnosophists*, Athenaeus tells a story in which a ship en route to Egypt encounters a violent storm. The sailors prayed to a statue of Aphrodite. The goddess then caused branches of green myrtle to appear from the statue. The wonderful fragrance of the myrtle cured the sailors' seasickness, and the sun began to shine. When the ship landed safely, the captain consecrated the statue and the myrtle branches at the temple of Aphrodite, and held a banquet at the temple, giving everyone who attended a myrtle garland.

Perhaps less familiar than the relationship between myrtle and Aphrodite is the relationship between myrtle and death. In Euripides's *Elektra*, Elektra says her father's grave is dishonored because it hasn't been sprayed with myrtle. Later, an old man loyal to Agamemnon, Elektra's father, places myrtle sprigs by his grave. Gold myrtle wreaths of extraordinary workmanship have been discovered by archaeologists at multiple burial sites in Greece, primarily in central Macedonia, dating from the fourth century BCE. Scholars debate whether these wreaths were worn to avert evil spirits, as symbols of rank, or to designate the wearer as someone who had been initiated in the rites of the Eleusinian Mysteries, the sacred rites celebrating the reunion of Demeter and Persephone (*see* "Barley").

In fact, myrtle wreaths were worn by priests, priestesses, and torchbearers at the Eleusinian Mysteries. Initiates in the mysteries are often depicted holding myrtle staffs. It seems especially appropriate that a plant related to both love and death features so prominently in the mysteries, which celebrated the love of Demeter and Persephone, and also promised a kinder death (life in Hades) for those who were initiated.

Theophrastus tells us that both the leaves and fruit of myrtle were used to make perfumes and says that the fruit has a taste like wine. He also offers copious advice on how to propagate, plant, and grow myrtle. In *De Materia Medica*, Dioscorides recommends myrtle for spitting blood, scorpion stings, and dandruff.

In fact, modern research confirms the effectiveness of myrtle in controlling dandruff and the itch that comes with it. Different parts of the myrtle plant have also proven to be anti-inflammatory, are high in antioxidants, and have antimicrobial properties. It is not widely used in Western medicine, but research is ongoing.

As a garden plant, myrtle is an evergreen tree or shrub that usually grows to be about ten feet tall. It is hardy to USDA Zones 8–10. Flowers are fragrant, white or pale pink in color, and slightly more than an inch in diameter, with multiple, showy stamens that give the blooms a delicate, fuzzy appearance. This is a stunning plant in bloom, worthy of the beautiful Aphrodite. The flowers are edible and can be added to salads. The fruit is edible, too, and is the essential ingredient in mirto liqueur, a traditional Sardinian digestif with a wonderful flavor that is both fruity and herbal.

Perhaps the gap between love and death isn't so big after all. Phaedra killed herself because of forbidden love, and the men in *Lysistrata* swore they'd die if they didn't have sex immediately. When Dionysus descended to Hades to liberate his mother, Semele (*see* "Fig"), he brought myrtle as a gift to trade for his mother. They emerged from the underworld at the future site of Troezen, where the cursed and desperate Phaedra mutilated myrtle leaves and lusted fatally for Hippolytus.

LOVE POTIONS AND LIBIDO KILLERS

Lettuce

Chaste Tree

Myrrh

Quince

Lettuce

Lactuca spp.

Today lettuce is a salad green. More than two thousand years ago it was the deathbed of Adonis (lover of Aphrodite) and a symbol of impotence.

Why was a plant associated with Adonis, most beautiful of men and paramour of the goddess of love, also a symbol of impotence? Surely Adonis and Aphrodite were having sex night and day. As with most Greek myths, there are multiple versions of the story, but all of them include the premature death of Adonis. Some stories describe him as too young to have a beard, and Bion (a second-century BCE pastoral poet) calls him Aphrodite's boy-husband. But Aphrodite wasn't only Adonis's much more mature lover, she was also responsible for his birth.

Adonis was a child of incest, born from the myrrh tree (*see* "Myrrh"). His mother, Myrrha, was turned into the plant when she begged to be removed from both the living and the dead as punishment for seducing her father. She was mightily ashamed and had no idea that her behavior was due to a curse from Aphrodite. Myrrha was pregnant at the time of her transformation into the myrrh tree, and when Adonis was ready to be born, he emerged from the bark of that tree.

Aphrodite claimed baby Adonis and sent him to the underworld to be raised by Persephone, wife of Hades. Some say she sent him there so no one else would see how beautiful he was. When Aphrodite came to collect him, Persephone refused to give him up; she had fallen in love with the handsome boy. Zeus decreed that Adonis should spend one third of the year with Persephone, one third with Aphrodite, and one third with whomever he chose. He chose Aphrodite (big surprise), and so spent eight months every year with her, and four months every year in the underworld, a living human among the dead.

While Adonis brought Aphrodite much joy, he was also the source of much sorrow. Adonis died while still a boy, gored by a wild boar. Some say Ares sent the boar because he was jealous. (He and Aphrodite had history.) Others say the boar was sent by Apollo or Artemis as punishment for offenses Aphrodite committed against them. Regardless of whoever sent the boar, Adonis died on a bed of lettuce, and after that, lettuce was associated with death.

But why was lettuce also a symbol of impotence? So many reasons:

» Adonis was gored by the boar in the groin, implying impotence as well as rendering him dead.
» Adonis's lack of skills as a hunter made him effeminate in the eyes of the ancient Greeks.
» Because Adonis had never procreated, he was not considered manly. Sappho describes him as delicate.
» Dioscorides says that lettuce is cool by nature, i.e., not sexy.
» Pliny the Elder tells us that one type of lettuce (called eunuch by the Pythagoreans) quenches sexual appetites. (The Pythagoreans believed sex was a distraction that should be tightly controlled.)

By the transitive property of impotence: Adonis = lettuce = not macho.

In Athenian comedy, Greek men rejected lettuce as food, fearing it would make them unable to perform. A fragment of the fourth-century BCE comedy *Ialemos* (by the poet Amphis) is one among several comedic warnings about the effects of eating lettuce on sexual prowess.

A curse upon destructive lettuces! When attempting intercourse with a woman, if someone not yet sixty years old should eat them, he would toss and turn the whole night long without accomplishing even a single one of his desires, rubbing off with his hand his doom imposed by fate instead of rendering his services.

Is it possible the men of ancient Greece were jealous of Adonis? Did they demean him because he was so handsome and the chosen lover of Aphrodite? Did they wish *they* could consort with the goddess of love? While men ridiculed Adonis and refused to eat lettuce, ancient Greek women considered the plant not only useful, but useful specifically in relation to *fertility*. Go figure: The same plant that sapped men of their fertility improved the fertility of women. Dioscorides recommended it to regulate menstruation and to improve lactation. And while Hebe (goddess of youth) is usually considered the daughter of Hera and Zeus, an alternate origin myth says that in revenge for Zeus's giving birth to Athena on his own, Hera conceived Hebe alone, by eating lettuce.

In any case, lettuce was an essential ingredient in the gardens of Adonis, which were planted as part of the Adonia, an annual celebration at which women mourned Adonis's death. In the heat of summer, they planted seeds in pottery and carried the dish gardens up to their rooftops where the seeds quickly sprouted in the heat and bright sun. Just as quickly, the sprouts died, thanks to the aforementioned heat and bright sun. Like Adonis, who died before maturity, the plants in the pottery gardens bore no fruit.

Most men saw the Adonia as rowdy and licentious, claiming only prostitutes and courtesans celebrated. They ridiculed the short-lived gardens, coining the proverb "more fruitless than the gardens of Adonis."

In Plato's *Phaedrus*, Socrates juxtaposes the fruitless containers of seedlings with serious farming. He considers the gardens of Adonis to be beautiful (like Adonis himself) but also frivolous (again, like Adonis).

But for the women of Athens, the Adonia was far from frivolous. Women's lives were basically restricted to their homes; if they were allowed out, it was only to perform certain limited duties, including mourning at public funerals. Yet in the sixth century BCE, the Athenian lawgiver Solon decided that public mourning was unseemly for women, and he limited their role as official funeral mourners, isolating them even further. The Adonia allowed women to gather again, ostensibly to perform a traditionally female task (mourning), but more importantly to commune with their neighbors, to converse and confide. Some scholars speculate mourning for Adonis allowed these women to mourn their own losses: parents, husbands, and children. They celebrated community while planting lettuce.

Most modern herbalists use lettuce (*Lactuca* spp.) extract for pain relief and as a soporific. The medicine is made as a double extraction, first in alcohol, then in water. A few herbalists still consider it a treatment for nymphomania and priapism, echoing the plant's ancient uses.

Today, lettuce is an easy-to-grow, cool weather vegetable, devoid of links to sex and impotence. Gardeners can choose from beautiful, bicolored red leaf lettuce, sturdy romaine, crunchy iceberg, or heirloom deer tongue lettuce, to name just a few. Lettuce matures quickly, with most varieties going from seed to harvest in under two months. But lettuce bolts fast in hot weather, becoming bitter and tough, so plant it in early spring and in fall, when cool growing temperatures produce a tastier, more tender crop. Then make yourself a delicious Greek salad and remember unfortunate Adonis.

Chaste Tree

Vitex agnus-castus

The name pretty much says it all, right? And yet uses of the chaste tree in ancient Greece ranged from quenching sexual desire to beating naked young men as they attempted to steal cheese. As fascinating as that last scenario sounds, let's first look at the chaste tree as an anaphrodisiac, a plant that suppresses sexual urges.

The Thesmophoria was a Panhellenic festival celebrating Demeter, Persephone, and fertility. It was three days long and reserved for married citizen women only. No children (except nursing babies), no virgins, and most scholars agree, no slaves or courtesans. Only sexually well-behaved women were allowed to participate. Details of the festival were kept secret, and little is known today about the specifics of the celebration. We know that the women camped in tents with minimal furniture, they fasted, and they engaged in ritual obscenity, telling crude jokes related to sex. The goal was to promote fertility, both relating to grain (the festival was held in fall, when seeds were sown for winter crops) and to the family.

Before and during the Thesmophoria, women abstained from sex. First, they needed to be "pure" to celebrate the goddesses, and second, many cultures believed that abstaining from sex resulted in increased fertility once abstention came to an end. The chaste tree was also sacred to Hera, and as the goddess of marriage and childbirth, it became associated with fertility and sex within the confines of marriage.

Yet despite this connection to fertility, the chaste tree was considered an anaphrodisiac and was used in this way at the Thesmophoria. When the women fasted, they sat on mats woven from the branches of the chaste tree. According to Pliny the Elder, they also slept on chaste tree leaves. Not only was this a physical reminder of the need for chastity, but it was also believed that the plant had the power to prevent unchaste thoughts. Remember, ancient Athenian men thought ancient Athenian women were a bunch of randy wenches, just waiting to run wild at the first opportunity. Encouraging chastity was very important . . . at least to the men.

We don't hear much about women in Spartan culture. They were allowed to exercise publicly (in the nude, just like the men) and to compete in athletics. Sounds fair, right? But once Spartan women were of marrying age, things got tricky. Their husbands could loan them out to produce offspring for other men, and the wedding night involved ritual kidnapping, shaving the bride's head, and dressing her up like a man to await her husband in the dark. After the deed was done, the husband returned to his barracks, visiting his wife for sex on occasion, but continuing to live and eat with his male contemporaries.

Most of what we know about Sparta revolves around their fierce male warriors who valued loyalty, the ability to tolerate hardship, and absolute commitment to the city-state. They were very different from the Athenians, whose contributions to theater, rhetoric, and philosophy are still recognized today. The Spartans were doers, not talkers, and their customs often seem bizarre and sometimes cruel. Take, for example, their annual, ritual flogging of young men.

Xenophon tells us that Spartan boys were given one article of clothing per year—which may be why they spent so much time in the nude. They were also encouraged to steal food, not only because the Spartans

enforced a meager diet, but also because the ability to successfully raid an enemy's supplies was a valuable skill. In *Moralia*, Plutarch describes the customs of the Spartans, including how adolescent boys were flogged at the altar of Artemis Orthia (a special, Spartan version of Artemis), vying to be the one who could tolerate the greatest number of blows. Put together the thieving and the flogging and we arrive at The Stealing of the Cheeses.

At the sanctuary of Artemis Orthia in Sparta, cheese was piled on the altar and guarded by adult men with whips made from chaste tree branches. Chaste tree branches are slim and flexible; they make excellent switches. Adolescent boys stole as much cheese as they could, while being chased and flogged by their elders. Punishment was administered not for stealing, but for stealing *badly*, teaching the boys to become better thieves.

The flexibility of chaste tree branches not only made them excellent whips, but also made them useful as fasteners, as when Apollo attempted to bind young Hermes (who had stolen Apollo's cattle), or when Odysseus tied his men underneath the Cyclops's sheep to escape his cave (*see* "Olive"), or when the pirates tried to shackle Dionysus (*see* "Ivy") in their unsuccessful kidnapping attempt.

But the chaste tree was useful for more than just its branches. Pliny the Elder lists thirty-three remedies made from the plant including a treatment for flatulence, an antidote for serpent and spider venom, and a freckle remover. In *Materia Medica*, Dioscorides describes the seed as being like pepper. He suggests it helps with lactation and menstrual flow, and Hippocrates suggests multiple ways it can be used to assist with conception, which was the single most important job of women in ancient Greece. Today, medicinal uses of the chaste tree are primarily related to female biology. Herbalists may prescribe it to relieve symptoms of PMS and menopause, but as of yet, no broad, controlled clinical trials have confirmed the chaste tree's efficacy in this area.

The chaste tree is a lovely garden plant, with spikes of purple flowers and a shrubby growth habit. It's reliably hardy to USDA Zone 7 and can survive in Zone 6 with winter protection. Unfortunately, its leaves resemble those of cannabis, and stories abound in the horticultural community about concerned citizens narcing on their neighbors, who wake up to find the police in their gardens, armed with loppers and shovels. At least there are no naked boys with stolen cheeses in the backyard. That would be hard to explain.

Myrrh

Commiphora myrrha

As with many Greek myths, there are variations of the story of Myrrha, but none of them end well. At least not for Myrrha. While storytellers do not agree on whether she was born in Cyprus or Assyria, and whether she was named Myrrha or Smyrna, they do agree that she was a beautiful girl and that either her mother or father angered Aphrodite by bragging that Myrrha was more beautiful than the goddess. Did Myrrha walk around tossing her hair and telling everyone how beautiful she was? No, she did not. But when the gods are angry, they do not hesitate to punish broadly; Myrrha paid a terrible price for her parent's hubris.

Many suitors vied for Myrrha's hand, but she rejected them all, because Aphrodite's curse had caused Myrrha to fall in love with her own father, Cinryas. Ovid's version of the story claims it was one of the Furies who cursed Myrrha, not Aphrodite. But Ovid gives no reason why the Furies would be angry with Myrrha so let's blame Aphrodite, who never appreciated competition.

Myrrha herself was horrified by her feelings of lust for her father. She reproached herself as perverted, as a whore, and she considered fleeing the country. Finally, she decided to kill herself. But just as she prepared her noose, her nurse wrenched the rope from Myrrha's neck. She quickly guessed that Myrrha was in love, but Myrrha would not divulge the name of the man she desired.

When at last her nurse realized that Myrrha was in love with her father, she tried desperately to dissuade Myrrha. Neither of them knew this was the result of Aphrodite's curse but it would have made no difference if they had. Since when does the Goddess of Love listen to reason? Myrrha had two choices: She could kill herself or she could sleep with her father. The nurse's love for Myrrha overcame her revulsion at incest, and she decided to make the match.

During the Thesmophoria, married women were forbidden to lay with their husbands for nine days, and Myrrha's mother had left her husband's bed for the duration. The nurse approached Cinryas and explained that a young woman she knew was passionately in love with him. To conceal Myrrha's identity, the nurse brought Myrrha to her father's bed in total darkness, where they did the deed. This was repeated for several nights until Cinryas's curiosity got the best of him and he lit a lamp. When he saw his lover was his daughter he drew his sword and chased her into the night.

Myrrha fled her home, crossing Arabia, pregnant with her father's child. She begged the gods for help, asking them to remove her from both the world of the living and the world of the dead so that her crime would not shame either one. Some say Aphrodite had pity on Myrrha, but more often it was said that an unnamed deity heard Myrrha's pleas and turned her into the myrrh tree. Myrrha's tears are the resinous drops the tree exudes, giving us fragrant myrrh. And Myrrha's child, Adonis, was born from the body of the tree.

In ancient times, myrrh was considered especially useful for producing visions and prophetic dreams. The Greek magical papyri are a group of documents found in Egypt, written primarily in ancient Greek between 200 BCE and 400 CE. They give recipes for magic spells to bring visions, ecstatic states, prophecies, communication with the gods, and to attract a lover. Many of these spells include myrrh, which is either consumed, burned as incense, or applied to the body.

Myrrh is best known for its presence in the New Testament as a baby shower gift. It didn't grow in Greece, but was a valued item traded with what is now Yemen and Somalia. Because the plant is difficult to cultivate outside of its native range, the supply of myrrh has always been limited. This, combined with the fact that it was considered something of a panacea, made myrrh a valuable commodity.

Historically myrrh has been used in food, as a medicine, in embalming, as a fragrance, and in incense. Today myrrh is used in toothpaste, incense, cosmetics, and pain relievers. It is even being studied for chemotherapy and wound healing because of its antiseptic and antitumor properties. Myrrh is still harvested the same way it has been for millennia: The branches and trunk are sliced to allow a gummy sap to ooze out, which then hardens into transparent, fragrant balls of resin.

Because of its very specific cultural requirements, myrrh has never been a successful garden plant. Some people grow it today as a houseplant, most often as a bonsai, where its thorny, twisted shape is appreciated as ornamental. Myrrh is very picky about watering; this is not a houseplant for beginners.

Poor Myrrha never had a chance. But vengeful Aphrodite did not escape unscathed. She eventually fell madly in love with Adonis (*see* "Lettuce"), and her heart was broken when he died as a young man. Some might say Aphrodite got what she deserved.

Quince

Cydonia oblonga

Would you recognize a quince if you saw one? Today the quince is a novelty fruit, but in ancient Greece the quince was appreciated as a food, a valuable trade item, an aphrodisiac, and the central object in several well-known myths. In fact, the quince may have been the golden apple that started the Trojan War (*see* "Apple"). "How's that?" you ask. Well, it's a member of the apple family, it's always golden in color (unlike apples, which are sometimes yellow and sometimes green but most often red), and it's better suited to the growing climate of Greece than apples. Need more convincing? While the word μηλο (pronounced meelo) means apple in modern Greek, that was not the case in ancient Greek. In ancient Greek μηλον (pronounced meelon) referred to *all* tree fruits except nuts, just as the word *corn* once described all grains in British English. So translating the ancient Greek μηλον as our modern *apple* isn't always correct.

For his eleventh labor, Herakles was tasked to retrieve golden fruit from the Garden of the Hesperides, at the edge of the known world. The trees had been a wedding gift from Gaia (Mother Earth) to Hera and

Zeus and they were guarded by Atlas, his daughters, and a fierce dragon. Some scholars claim these golden fruits were citrus, perhaps because the word for *citrus* in modern Greek is almost identical to the word for the Hesperides and is therefore reminiscent of the garden where the golden fruit grew. But citrus was unknown in Greece until Alexander brought it back from Mesopotamia, several hundred years after the original golden fruit myths were recorded. Most classicists today agree that the golden fruit was actually the quince.

When Herakles freed Prometheus from his millennia-long torture (*see* "Fennel"), Prometheus thanked Herakles by telling him how to obtain the golden fruit and accomplish his eleventh labor. He must first find Atlas, who holds the world on his shoulders just outside the garden walls. Herakles would hold the world for Atlas, while Atlas went into the garden and obtained the golden fruit. All went as planned until Atlas realized he'd been released from a terrible burden—one he was not eager to resume. He offered to deliver the fruit for Herakles. Herakles pretended to agree, but asked Atlas to just hold the world for one minute so Herakles could adjust his cloak as padding for his shoulder. When Atlas took the world back, Herakles picked up the fruit and left.

In addition to being sacred to Hera, the quince was sacred to Aphrodite, primarily because it may have been the golden apple that led to the Trojan War. As a tree fruit with many seeds, it was also considered a symbol of fertility and it was known for its sweet fragrance and flavor, which Greeks believed gave the fruit powers as an aphrodisiac. In Plutarch's *Moralia*, he tells us that Solon instructed brides to nibble on a quince before getting into bed on their wedding night, to sweeten their breath and make them more appealing to their new grooms.

In the story of Kydippe and Akontius, the quince was used to force an unwilling lover to accept an unwelcome marriage proposal. For Akontius it was love at first sight, but not for Kydippe. Akontius, a self-admitted stalker, followed Kydippe and her nurse as they entered the temple of Artemis. He picked a quince fruit from a nearby tree and wrote on it, "By Artemis, it is Acontius I shall wed." Then he tossed the

inscribed quince into the temple where the nurse picked it up. But the nurse couldn't read, so she handed the fruit to Kydippe, who read the inscription out loud. Since she was in a holy temple, her words were considered a sacred vow.

But Kydippe was already betrothed. She fell ill on her wedding day, causing the ceremony to be postponed. This happened again and again, and after the third time, Kydippe's father asked the oracle at Delphi for advice. The oracle told him that Artemis was punishing his daughter for breaking her vow, and that Kydippe must marry Akontius. Apparently, the promise made to Kydippe's betrothed was irrelevant, not having been made in a sacred precinct.

Ovid elaborates on the story in *Heroides*, where he wrote imagined letters between Kydippe and Akontius. Here, Akontius does some classic victim-blaming, claiming that if he did anything wrong it's Kydippe's fault for being so beautiful. He threatens to take her by force and in the end Kydippe relents. Akontius doesn't seem the slightest bit concerned that his love is not reciprocated: "You may chide and be angry as much as you will, if only you let me enjoy you while you are angry." What a romantic.

The earliest traces of quince cultivation in Greece date to 600 BCE and the port of Kydonia (modern-day Chania) on the northwestern coast of Crete. The fruit was called the Cydonian apple, and some historians believe it was named after the port town, which served as a gateway for exporting the fruit throughout Europe.

So how does such a delicious fruit with such an interesting history fall out of favor? Perhaps it's the quince's appearance that puts people off. It's large, lumpy, and initially covered with white fuzz, which mostly disappears as the fruit ripens. Or maybe it's the challenge of getting quinces to ripen outside of their native habitat. In warm climates with long growing seasons quinces may ripen to be soft and pleasant to eat when raw. But in cooler climates, the fruit often doesn't have time to fully ripen before frost hits. These quinces are hard and intensely sour, requiring cooking to make them delicious.

Quinces produce fragrant, pale pink flowers in early spring; they may require protection from late frosts in some areas. They grow best in full sun and fertile, moist, well-drained soils. Leave quince fruits on the tree as long as possible, letting them turn from green to yellow, and giving the fuzz time to disappear. If frost threatens, harvest any that are almost ripe, and let them ripen on the kitchen counter, but only if they're already showing some yellow color. Fully green quinces will not ripen off the tree.

Sure, quinces require more work to make them palatable than the average apple does. But a ripe quince is worth the effort. Even if you're not planning to use one to entrap an unwilling lover.

Epilogue

Why are these stories so memorable? Do we wish there really were a fruit that could make us forget our sorrows, our fears, our regrets? Would we like to use cannabis to commune with the dead? Tell Mum you miss her? Tell Dad you're grateful for everything he did for you? Are these things possible? Not really. But it's fun to imagine what it would be like to harness the magical powers of these mythic plants.

Were there really twelve Olympian gods in human form living at the top of Mount Olympus? I've been there and can report I saw only a few fellow hikers and an astonishingly agile dachshund. Mythology isn't real, but at its best it contains elements of truth, and *that's* why it stays with us. We may never need to carry a burning coal in a fennel stalk, but once you see that plant in the wild and you know the story of Prometheus, you say, "Yeah, I see how that could work." The story makes the lesson stick.

So what will you do with what you've learned? Will you become an herbalist and use myrtle leaves to control your dandruff? Will you remember the lesson of Baucis and Philemon and always welcome a stranger in need? Will you explain to your children that Shakespeare borrowed from the story of Pyramus and Thisbe when he wrote *Romeo and Juliet*?

You don't actually have to *do* anything. These stories have lives of their own, and once you've heard them, they're hard to forget. They bubble up when you pick fresh lettuce from your garden or taste a pine-scented retsina on a hot summer day. The gardens of the gods are still alive after thousands of years. They survive in art, in mythology, and in our minds. As do the lessons learned from mythic plants.

APPENDIX:

Ancient Authors

The following list is by no means complete, but includes all the authors mentioned in Mythic Plants. *Dates are approximate.*

Aeschylus (circa 524–456 BCE): Greek tragic playwright sometimes called the father of tragedy; author of the *Oresteia*, and *Prometheus Bound*, among others

Amphis (fourth century BCE): Comic Athenian playwright; only fragments of his work survive

***Anacreontea*, the** (circa first century BCE to the fifth to sixth century CE): a group of lyric poems composed in the style of Anacreon, a Greek lyric poet of the sixth to fifth century BCE who wrote primarily about love and wine

Apollonius of Rhodes (first half of the third century BCE): Greek author of epic poetry, best known for the *Argonautica*

Apuleius (second century CE): Latin writer and philosopher, author of *The Golden Ass*

Aristophanes (444–386 BCE): Greek playwright of Old Comedy (initial phase of ancient Greek comedy), especially known for his political satire and his seriously raunchy innuendos; author of *Lysistrata, Peace,* and *Clouds,* among others

Aristotle (384–322 BCE): Greek philosopher who also wrote on the natural sciences, including *History of Animals*

Athenaeus (second to third century CE): Greek author of *The Deipnosophists*, i.e., the dinner-table philosophers; the work refers to and quotes from multiple ancient authors whose works do not survive in any other form

Bion (second to first century BCE): Greek pastoral poet; only one complete poem of his survives, and it's a beauty: "Lament for Adonis"

Callimachus (third century BCE): Greek poet from Alexandria, Egypt, author of a "Hymn to Demeter"

Clement of Alexandria (circa 150–215 CE): early Christian theologian and proselytizer, venerated as a saint by some (but not all) Christian faiths

Diodorus Siculus (first century BCE): Greek historian, author of the *Bibliotheka Historica* (aka the *Library of History*), which covers more than a millennium of history; less than half of this work survives

Dioscorides (40–90 CE): Greek physician; author of *De Materia Medica*, a five-volume encyclopedia of medicine

Euripides (484–406 BCE): Greek playwright, best known for his tragedies including *Hippolytus*, and *Bacchae*, among others

Graves, Robert (1895–1985): translator of ancient Greek and Latin; author of *The Greek Myths*

Herodotus (484–425 BCE): Greek historian; author of *The History*, an account of the Persian War

Hesiod (circa 750–650 BCE): Greek poet; author of *Theogony* and *Works and Days*

Hippocrates (circa 460–370 BCE): Greek physician sometimes called the father of medicine; the Hippocratic Collection (*Corpus Hippocraticum*) includes many works now considered to have been written by others at later dates, as well as some attributed to Hippocrates himself

Homer (late eighth century BCE): Greek poet in the oral tradition; author of the *Iliad* and the *Odyssey*; some scholars believe these two epic poems may have been written by two different authors

Hyginus (circa 1–100 CE): Latin author of the *Fabulae* (aka Stories), a collection of approximately three hundred myths

Linnaeus, Carl (1707–1778): Swedish biologist and physician; best known for formalizing the Latin binomial system of taxonomy used today

Menander (circa 342–290 BCE): Greek writer of New Comedy (mildly satiric view of contemporary Athenian society); none of his work survives in complete form

Nicander of Colophon (second century BCE): Greek poet who wrote about venomous animals, poisons, and their antidotes; best known for *Alexipharmaca*

Nonnus (fifth century CE): Greek epic poet best known as the author of the *Dionysiaca*, an epic poem about Dionysus

Ovid (43 BCE–circa 17 CE): Roman poet who wrote extensively about Greek mythology; best known for *Metamorphoses* and *Fasti*

Pausanias (110–180 CE): Greek geographer and author of *Description of Greece*, which describes ancient Greece from firsthand observation

Plato (428–347 BCE): Greek philosopher, student of Socrates, and teacher of Aristotle; best known for the *Republic*, *Phaedo*, and *Laws*, among others

Pliny the Elder (23–79 CE): Roman naturalist, philosopher, and author of *Natural History*, an encyclopedia of general knowledge; Pliny died attempting to rescue a friend from the eruption of Mount Vesuvius

Plutarch (46–119 CE): Greek philosopher and biographer; best known for *Moralia* and *Parallel Lives*, the latter a collection of biographies of famous Romans and Greeks

Pollen, Michael (1955–): author of *This Is Your Mind on Plants*

Proclus (circa 410–485 CE): Greek philosopher; primarily known for his commentaries on earlier philosophers and for his *Chrestomathy*, a collection of epic poems relating to the Trojan War

Rowling, J. K. (1965–): author of the Harry Potter books

Sappho (circa 630–570 BCE): Greek lyric poet from the island of Lesbos whose work mostly survives in fragments; best known for her love poetry

Servius (fourth century CE): Latin author best known for his commentary on Virgil

Sophocles (circa 497–406 BCE): Greek tragic playwright, the most celebrated of his time; author of *Antigone*, *Oedipus Rex*, and *Elektra*, among others

Soranus of Ephesus (first to second century CE): Greek physician; well-known for his treatise on gynecology

Statius (first century CE): Roman author of the *Achilleid*, an unfinished epic poem about Achilles

Theophrastus (371–287 BCE): Greek philosopher and the father of botany, who wrote extensively on the classification, descriptions, uses, and growth habits of plants; best known for *Enquiry into Plants*

Thucydides (circa 460–400 BCE): Greek historian and author of *History of the Peloponnesian War*, which describes the famous war between Athens and Sparta

Virgil (70–19 BCE): Roman poet and author of the epic poem the *Aeneid*

Xenophon (circa 430–355 BCE): Greek military leader and historian; he is best known for his historical writing including much about Spartan traditions

ACKNOWLEDGMENTS

As always, thanks to Michael and Elizabeth for endless reading of multiple drafts, and for their firm, intelligent, and always kind suggestions. And thanks to Emma Malinasky, my ancient Greek tutor, for help with translations and moments of epiphany. Many thanks also to my agent, Michelle Tessler, for finding a home for this book, and to my editor, Mary Ellen O'Neill, and her assistant, Julia Perry, for expert guidance through the editorial process. Thanks to Lisel Ashlock, a brilliant illustrator, who combines reality and fantasy in just the right proportions for a book about plants in mythology. And much appreciation to Reagan Ruff, for putting everything together into this beautiful package you hold in your hands.

Photo by Matthew Carasella

Ellen Zachos is a Harvard graduate, a former
Broadway performer, and a Greek American horticulturist
who enjoys nothing more than regaling anyone who will listen with stories about fascinating plants. She is the author of
ten previous books about plants and has been recognized by
Garden Communicators International for both her writing
and podcasting. Ellen has been chosen as a Great American
Gardener by the EPCOT International Flower & Garden
Festival and speaks at horticultural organizations both nation-
ally and internationally. For six years she was the co-host of
the *Plantrama* podcast, which ranked in the top fifty home
and garden podcasts nationwide, and she was also an instruc-
tor at the New York Botanical Garden for fifteen years. Ellen
now lives in Santa Fe, New Mexico.

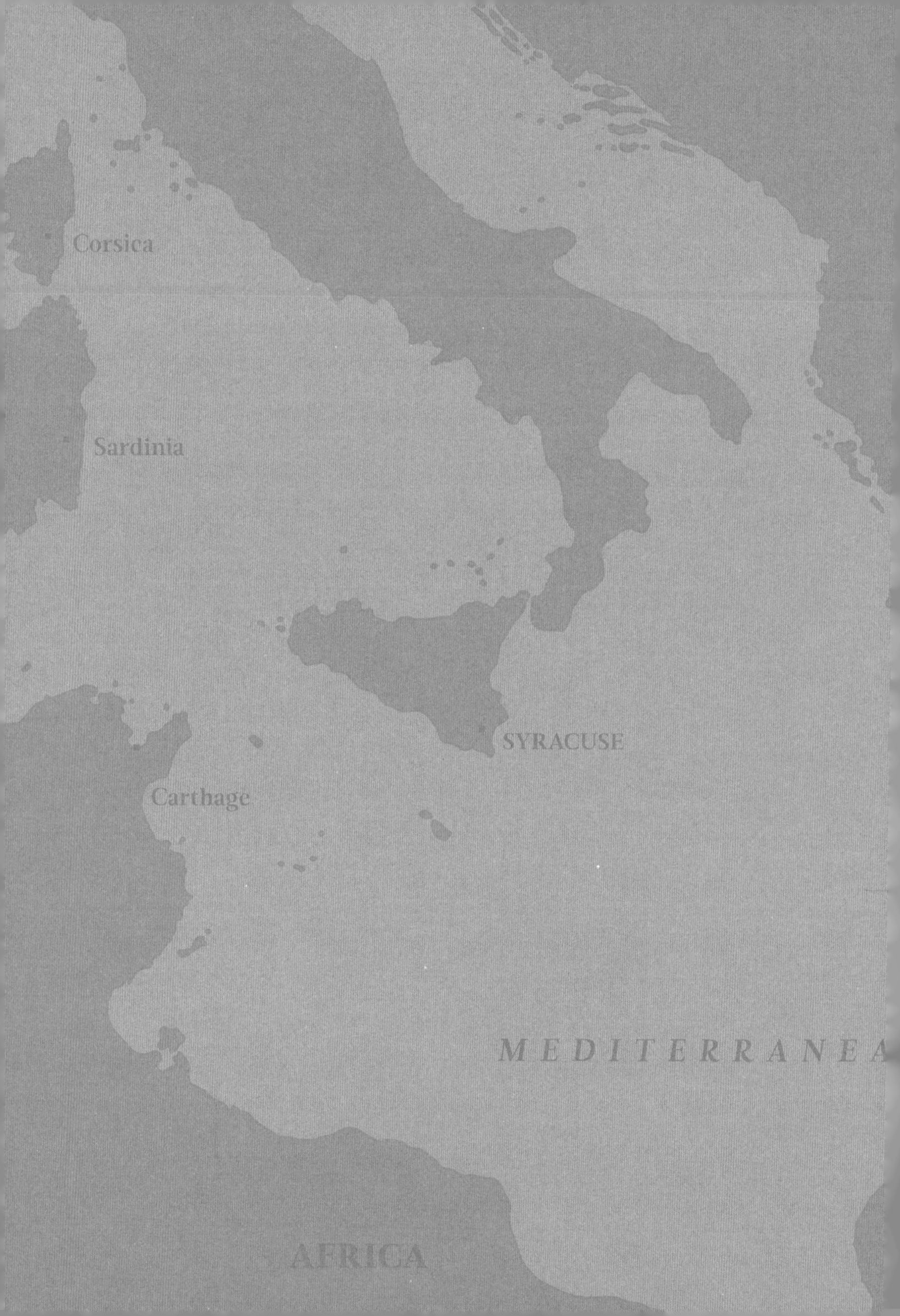
Corsica
Sardinia
SYRACUSE
Carthage
MEDITERRANEA
AFRICA